MOM
IS *Not* ALWAYS
RIGHT

KENDRA
ARAUJO

PUBLISHING

Published by:
Capucia, LLC
211 Pauline Drive #513
York, PA 17402
www.capuciapublishing.com

Paperback ISBN: 978-1-945252-96-9
eBook ISBN: 978-1-945252-97-6
Library of Congress Control Number: 2020925311

Layout: Ranilo Cabo
Editor and Proofreader: Catherine Wineberg
Book Midwife: Carrie Jareed

Printed in the United States of America

DOWNLOAD THE WORKBOOK FREE!

READ THIS FIRST

Just to say thanks for buying this book

(or thinking about buying this book)

I would like to give you the Workbook 100% FREE!

TO DOWNLOAD, GO TO:

www.momisnotalwaysright.com/resources/

Start designing your rebel lifestyle—

a life fully on YOUR terms—NOW!

CONTENTS

REBEL LIFESTYLE DESIGN STEP 2
RADICAL CLARITY   **159**

REBEL LIFESTYLE DESIGN STEP 3
TAKE ACTION   **355**

Dedication

TO MY MOM

Tú me hiciste la mujer que soy ahora. Aun con las rebeldías, ir en contra de lo que tu querías para mi en casi todo y pasar la mayoría de los años de mi adolescencia peleadas, todo lo que he aprendido de la vida, de ser una mujer fuerte, plena y exitosa, y sobre todo de ser una mujer libre viene de lo que me enseñaste, ya sea directa o indirectamente. Este libro es prueba de que si soy quien soy, es por ti. Te amo. Gracias por aguantarme y por hacer tu mejor esfuerzo para que yo me convierta en un ser humano bondadoso y responsable. Y mientras escribo esto y no puedo parar de llorar, quiero que sepas que de ser mamá, quisiera ser como tú. Eres una gran mujer y un ejemplo a seguir.

TO MY DAD

Gracias papá por siempre estar ahí, por tener la mejor actitud conmigo y mis rebeldías, y sobre todo por trabajar tanto por sacarnos adelante. Por no darte por vencido cuando las cosas se pusieron difíciles, y por sacarme adelante en mi educación y en mi vida. No hay una hija más afortunada que yo por tenerte a ti de papá. ¡Gracias por todo daddy!

TO MY HUSBAND

Este día no sería posible sin ti, mi motor, mi soporte emocional, sentimental, social..., mi confidente, mi todo. Tú me impulsas e inspiras a ser mejor cada día, me motivas a que siga adelante aún cuando las cosas se ven difíciles, y también estás ahí para decirme cuando la estoy regando- o estoy "en la luna". Pero sobretodo, nunca, ni por un segundo, dudas de todo lo que puedo lograr, aun cuando yo esté dudando. Gracias por creer en todos mis sueños locos, confiar en mi los tuyos y por co-crear conmigo esta aventura. Entre risas y corajes para siempre. Gracias por existir.

TO YOU

Thank you for being here right now. Thank you for trusting me with your time, resources, and for joining this mission to help every woman in the world break free from expectations and start living her best life. If it weren't for you, this mission wouldn't be possible. I will never stop being grateful to you.

Letter to YOU, Rebel Reader

Dear Rebel,

As I'm on the final stages of publishing this book (and hopefully transforming the lives of countless women like you around the world), I wanted to take a moment to write you a few lines.

You see, this whole book exists because of you.

I was thinking about you when I wrote it. You were my sole inspiration. My end goal is that your life transforms for the better thanks to reading this book. Hopefully, just hopefully, this book inspires you so much that you take action on what you learn and even decide to share it with someone else.

In an effort to make your reading experience the best possible, I wanted to give you some advice on how to navigate this book that was written just for you.

First, understand that the main goal of this book is to get you from where you are in your life to where you want to be in realizing your dreams and becoming your happiest yet. Each chapter builds upon the previous one, so my first suggestion would be to read it in sequence.

Having said that, suggestion two is for you to start the first challenge while you are still reading the book. There is something magical about instant gratification! So, even though I suggest you read the book in sequence, feel free to start working on the first challenge today!

I know, I know, you are a rebel as am I, and you want to read what you want to read... but trust me on this; there is a reason I organized the chapters in this way and why I'm suggesting you start the challenge now; I have only your best interests in mind. ;)

Now, I don't want you to feel pressured to move at a fast pace trying to sprint your way chapter after chapter or to finish the whole thing for that matter. Suggestion three is not to feel the need to finish this book all at once just for the sake of finishing it.

"Did she just tell me not to finish reading her own book?"

Girl, you and I, we are rebels and we don't do things like other people do. This book is no different. This is not a book for you to sprint through, close, and then move on to the next one. You wouldn't be doing yourself a favor in doing so and this book is all about you doing what is right FOR YOU.

With that in mind, I have divided this book into three sections. The first two walk you through two different transformations.

The first section: Unconditional Self-Love is going to act as your foundation. It's all about taking internal action toward becoming the most authentic, courageous, and true version of yourself.

The second section: Radical Clarity builds on that foundation to guide you through the steps you need to take to see clearly and start designing your dream life — your own rebel lifestyle.

The third section: Rebel Lifestyle Design in Action contains the challenges.

As I mentioned before, I suggest working on the first challenge while you are still reading the book instead of getting all the way to the end to start making changes.

I hope you read the first section first while going through the first challenge and you let all that knowledge and self-discovery sink in before jumping into the second section.

Once you feel like you are ready (could be the next day, could be the next month), pick up the book again and brace yourself to take this world by storm as you start moving forward toward your dreams and to take some serious action. Read section two while simultaneously working on the second challenge.

My fourth suggestion is a little bit more of a request.

I want to ask of you the same thing I ask my workshop attendees and my listeners. If you have been following along, you know my one and only rule: No judging.

The first thing we tend to do as we are faced with new, challenging information is to judge. That could mean judging the information itself, the person delivering that information, or—more often than not—judging ourselves.

As you are facing the different prompts in this book, keep in mind that you are doing wonderfully. If you get it right the first time, or it takes you 10 or 100 tries, honor your process, honor yourself, and know that it too took me more than once to learn everything I'm sharing.

If you are feeling like you need extra support, come join us in the community at *http://www.momisnotalwaysright.com/resources* where some fellow rebels and I show up for each other and share love and support. Think of it as your tribe of rebel sisters.

Finally, as I finish writing this letter to you, I realize I can't express how excited I am for this journey you are about to begin.

I am here rooting for you, holding a glass of champagne, and toasting to your success.

Cheers,

Kendra Araujo

CHAPTER 1

My Why

As I'm writing this, I'm sitting in the coziest nook decorated in a blend of traditional and modern Turkish style. I'm looking out into the Bosphorus and the busy Besiktas neighborhood from our complimentary upgraded suite at the W hotel Istanbul.

I actually shouldn't be writing. I should be packing my bag since we need to head to the airport in about 45 min for our trip to Cairo to have an out-of-this-world encounter with one of the wonders of the world: the Giza Pyramids; however, I realize this moment right now is a huge part of why I travel and why traveling makes me feel fully alive—so I want to use it to help you to understand what this book will give you.

It's hard to put into words what this moment gives me. The complete peace and freedom from my window view, this amazing seat, this suite, the great coffee, this moment, and its equivalent in every country or city we go to are what motivate me to hop on a plane and seek this moment's experience again.

THIS IS WHAT A REBEL LIFESTYLE MEANS TO ME: FREEDOM. FREEDOM TO DO WITH MY LIFE WHATEVER I WANT.

Life is moving forward for all the people outside the window rushing to work, or friends, or home, or wherever they are going. I'm here to witness everyday life with the amazing ocean as a backdrop and realizing this is what I get to do with my life because I CHOSE to. This is what a rebel lifestyle means to me: Freedom. Freedom to do with my life whatever I want. That is exactly what I want for you.

When I was 14 years old and about to graduate junior high, I remember my friends and I were all excited to move on to high school. We had already done assignments with goal-setting questions like, "Where do you see yourself in 5 years," or "What do you want to be when you grow up," so we were pretty motivated to move forward with our lives and be "grownups."

For graduation day, the committee was putting together a slideshow with pictures of each graduate and we all had to write quotes for it. Instead of letting us write our own quotes, the nuns at my Catholic school handed us a paper with a list of some "fill in the blank" sentences to describe us: pet peeves, likes, etc. We each had to take the form home, complete it, and hand it in before graduation.

That evening, I started filling it out in the kitchen table and telling my mom about it while she was cooking dinner. It was all flowing well until we got to one question that would open my eyes to how the world worked, at least in my mom's head.

"What is your biggest dream?" I was quick to answer out loud, "Oh, that is easy! My life's biggest dream is to live life to the fullest!"

My mom dropped the spatula she was cooking with, turned around with a very surprised look on her face and said: "Kendra, that is not the answer... the answer is something like have a great career, live in a beautiful house, have a family..."

I replied, "Mom, that is all great and good, but my life's biggest dream is not that. I want to live life to the fullest! I want to experience as much as possible and miss out on almost nothing."

She still didn't get it, but decided it was not a big deal. For me, however, it was.

I remember this moment vividly as the moment I knew I wanted something different for my life. Different from what my mom expected of me or what she thought society expected of me.

I REMEMBER THIS MOMENT VIVIDLY AS THE MOMENT I KNEW I WANTED SOMETHING DIFFERENT FOR MY LIFE.

In this moment, I realized that, even though it probably was not going to be easy, I was going to do what I wanted, what made ME happy, and I wasn't going to let what anybody else thought stop me—even in a society where everyone is getting involved in everybody else's life.

My entire life, I have worked to fulfill the goal I set for myself at the end of 8th grade to "live life to the fullest." I have searched for new experiences and found what made me happy and fulfilled.

Growing up in Mexico, the reality behind "being a rebel," finding yourself, and putting yourself FIRST over your parents' expectations can quickly become a never-ending guilt-trip influenced by society and family with the stigma of being "selfish."

Even though your family is doing what they believe is in your best interest, it can end up crippling your personal growth if you don't make it out of their house fast enough; part of the Mexican tradition is living with your parents until you get married or leave for college. While this is more of a traditional situation, "society" enforces it if you let it.

When it was time to choose careers and colleges, I was fortunate to have good grades and access to the best schools in the country. My calculus teacher even asked me to apply for an engineering career; she was sure I'd get a scholarship!

I loved math...and problem solving... and even got straight As in my accounting and calculus classes; however, that wasn't what I wanted. No offense to anyone, but the idea of sitting behind a desk in a cubicle for the rest of my adult life sounded like the exact opposite of my dream life.

I wanted to travel and to experience the world and, as my mom would say, "Eat the world up in one bite." I searched and searched for a major that attracted me. I thought I'd found it when I learned

I could make a career in Image Design, also known as Fashion and Public Image Stylist.

As a fashion lover, and somewhat with an eye for what works and what doesn't, I thought, "This is a job I can do." I could spend my life telling public figures what to wear and how to act in public, charge big bucks, and get to have time freedom." The downside? The only school that offered this as an actual degree was in Spain.

The language was obviously not a barrier and maybe they offered some sort of scholarship since Mexican pesos to Euros is not exactly the best conversion rate; however, the main challenge I faced was the distance. In my parents' eyes, Barcelona was extremely far for me to go live on my own at 18, and, of course, the cost could be unbearable; plus, they were just afraid of me not being mature enough to handle it on my own.

Now, I'm going to be completely honest with you...mainly because I will ask you to be completely honest with me in a few pages and I believe trust is a two-way street. I also want to give you the whole picture.

Ninety percent of the reason I was looking into "outside the box" careers and schools that were far away was because I wanted to go as far away from home as possible. There—I said it.

Don't get me wrong; my life at home was really good. My parents loved me and supported me and my brothers are simply the best, most incredible friends and total confidantes. I couldn't help but feel, however, that if I didn't leave I was never going to find out who I really was, what I was really capable of, and—most importantly—I might never have had the courage to do it in front of my whole world.

There was something different about being a complete stranger in a new city where no one knows you and people won't judge you. Even more, they might judge from afar, but you won't care because you don't know them and their opinions don't bother you.

Mexican families are so close. I couldn't have been more blessed to grow up the way I did. Extended family and communities, however, do tend to meddle in everyone's business and comment and judge. That scrutiny gets to you as a teenage girl who is trying to feel accepted while at the same time trying to live life to the fullest.

I felt trapped in a world of "what will people say?" I needed a way out. I truly needed to experience life without the judging eyes of everyone around me. I needed to get to know *me* when no one was watching.

I FELT TRAPPED IN A WORLD OF "WHAT WILL PEOPLE SAY?"

It took a whole year for my parents to accept this (mainly because I refused to enroll in our local college for an entire year and instead got a job and started "throwing my future away"). In the end, they finally allowed me to go away for college and supported me the whole way.

I will forever be thankful for their support!!

Now I didn't go to Spain—the idea was a bit too much—but I did do a little bit of a soul searching and introspection. During that "sabbatical" year between high school and actually leaving for college, I researched all the possible majors I could take. While I loved telling people what to wear, not obtaining a degree was completely unacceptable to my parents, so I had to look for something that would end in a bachelor's degree.

I loved to cook as much as I liked math in school, however, the fear of one day hating it from doing it as a chore every day—and my mom's comments about how I was going to get super fat—killed the idea of going to Puebla in central Mexico.

Then I found interior design. I loved design and I thought I could do it. I loved the curriculum. One of the best schools in the country was in Guadalajara—a three-hour plane ride from home—so I said, "Let's go!" I sent in all my paperwork. My mom and I took a quick trip to visit the school. I was introduced to my entire extended family who lived in the city. I finally got the green light to move away from home and into my dream life.

When I arrived in this incredible city, and all the goodbyes had been said, I realized I was about to start living my dream! For the first time EVER, I was free to be whomever I wanted to be! I was free to do whatever I wanted to do and explore what made me curious! As long as I got good grades, I had my family's full support!

FOR THE FIRST TIME EVER, I WAS FREE TO BE WHOMEVER I WANTED TO BE! I WAS FREE TO DO WHATEVER I WANTED TO DO.

This was the first time I experienced that feeling of freedom that I mentioned earlier: the freedom that I have always searched for, the freedom that led me to write these words for you. I want you to experience that same freedom in your life: the freedom to be whomever you want to be and do whatever you truly want to do with whomever you want to do it... because girl, that freedom is possible for you just as it was possible for me.

It has been a few years since that first afternoon "living on my own" (which is an exaggeration since I was actually renting a room with a "host-family"), but I felt like all I had believed to this point was real. I COULD be anything I wanted. I COULD have this feeling of freedom and complete joy every single day of my life. I COULD fulfill all my dreams if I set my mind to it and if I worked hard. Most importantly, I COULD live a life defying the status quo in return for my utter happiness.

It's no surprise that a few years later, just as I was finishing up with school and right after graduation, I had no hesitation on our first date telling my now-husband Yahir what I wanted out of life. I had known my whole life that traveling was both the answer and the question in my life. That *being away* is a way of life, not just something you do on holidays or weekends.

I met my husband when I was 23 as I was graduating from the university. He was 33 and partying it up with a career already built. I always had a thing for guys a little older than I am. I always found I did not have a lot of things in common with guys my age; I guess I was always looking for something different—something more than college kids.

I remember our conversation turning serious quickly on that first date and we ended up sharing what our life goals truly were. The deal was to be completely honest with each other. If we liked what we saw, we would give it a real try. He cut to the chase and avoided games. I liked that A LOT!

My life goals were not typical. My truly honest if-this-happens-you-can-kill-me-now-and-I'll-die-happy life goal wasn't to get married, or be ultra-successful in my career, or make millions, or have kids... I did want the ocean front house like most of us, but my real goal in life, what I truly aspired to have for myself, was to travel.

I can feel the power in the words like I did back then. "I want to go everywhere. I want to try everything. I want to live everywhere. I want to see everything. I don't want children." What a powerful statement at my 23 years of age! I was so sure. I was also so lucky to be saying things like that to a man like Yahir.

His response was also powerful and honest. He said, "I want to travel, too and live in different places. I'm OK with no kids, however, I come as a package with my mom. One of my main goals in life is to make enough money to help her out on anything and everything."

I was so impressed by how much he loved his mom. He truly cared about her. He wanted to help her out, to make her feel safe and accompanied—even over the phone since she lives a couple of hours away.

We both agreed and almost immediately fell in love. He is such a good person and has such a good heart that not only did he take those words that we said to each other to himself, he has striven to make them a reality with me. He also pushes me to be a better person every day.

Even with all the plans, goals, and decisions, we struggled the first two years of our marriage to live outside the norm. Living outside the norm was not required for us to live happily and we did pretty much the usual things newlyweds do. We moved into a condo. Yahir had a 9 – 5 job. I got a part-time job while trying to re-launch my interior design business in our new city. Staying true to our dreams, we saved and took small weekend getaways and one-week vacations every six months, mainly using our anniversary as an excuse. (We had two weddings, so at least we had the chance to go out twice.)

One October afternoon, all the "normal" changed within minutes. Right after our first anniversary, I was at my part-time job doing my usual routine and Yahir called me to let me know he had been let go. I remember having mixed feelings from, "What do we do now?" to happiness that he was finally free of that job that made him miserable. Somehow, the one thing that I knew for sure was that we were going to be OK. My main goal at that point was that he, too, realized that we were going to be OK; we would simply get creative and find another source of income. The last thing I wanted was for him to get even more stressed out than when he had a job. Who would have thought this would be one of the best things that ever happened in our marriage?

This became a turning point in our relationship that led us on a path of self-discovery, teamwork, financial and time freedom, and lots and lots of traveling. This single event made us both stop and take a deep, long look at what we were doing and not doing, restructure our priorities on all aspects of our lives, feel closer than ever, and set new family goals with traveling as the ultimate way of living.

My main concern was to make sure Yahir didn't over-stress himself and that he realized that we were going to be OK. I've always been a glass half-full kind of woman, which allows me not to dwell so much on my problems, but rather to decide everything is going to work itself out somehow. In the end, it always has. There is no need to go on and on about a problem. Rather, move on to solving it, even if it's just you and your hopes working at it. This wasn't going to be the exception.

We sat down and looked at our options. To make it through this financial distress, we had to make some changes in our dynamic. In this moment, after a year of being married, we truly became a team. No more holdbacks. No more stupid fights over power. No more childish games. We became an all-in team ready to face the circumstances.

The next couple of months were hectic, but incredible! I was working six days a week in two different places, and loving most of it, while still trying to market my firm on my time off. Yahir was going to interviews like crazy while taking full responsibility for the house chores. While he did not love the chores, he was a full-on teammate! It was such a humbling and powerful experience. It changed us both and helped us reconnect with ourselves, with each other, and with our goals in life. Incredibly enough, these were the times that made us who we are as a couple today.

It's sometimes unbelievable how, when you are truly honest with yourself on what you want and what you expect out life, if you really feel it and put those things out for the universe (*The Secret* style), the opportunities come your way to make it all happen.

During this "financial crisis," we had an already-scheduled trip to New York. Spending New Year's Eve in New York had been on my bucket list for a long time. Something about the big city lights, ice skating in the park, and, of course, the big Times Square celebration with thousands of people, attracted me like crazy! Unfortunately, this particular year was not ending amazingly. Regardless, we had booked our flights in August and the hotel was paid. Also, Yahir could really use this mini-vacation to get his mind off things and I wanted to check it off my list! So, with our priorities clearly in place (our dreams first, in spite of our families thinking we were totally irresponsible), we decided to go.

Of course, we were on a budget, so I dedicated countless hours to researching for the greatest promotions, coming up with an itinerary and adding up the costs to see what was possible for us and what needed to be postponed for a second trip. During this research, I stumbled upon credit cards and their rewards points. One credit card offered 50,000 bonus points for signing up and double points on dining and travel. These points translated into over $625 to spend on everything related to travel including tours, entry tickets, transfer services from the airport, and lots of other fun stuff. This is exactly what I needed to keep us in budget and still be able to enjoy the Big Apple like we wanted!

With my mind made up, I signed up for the card and was on my way to discovering a brand new way of life: a life paid for with points. I had no idea it would be as fulfilling and as enjoyable to be able to travel the world paying most of it on rewards points or miles simply by doing your research and being loyal to your brands. This was only the beginning. My husband couldn't believe all we were able to afford on our budget and how much we had left for us. We ended up having an amazing time and it really opened my eyes to the world of credit card rewards.

It has been a few years since that trip. In the end, everything worked itself out with Yahir doing what he does best: owning a real estate firm. I got to sign big clients for my interior design business. Eventually, I decided to take a break from design to fulfill my passion of writing and helping others achieve their goals. Now we have been around the world twice for months straight— leaving everything behind—on what we call #araujosworldtour. We fly first and business class almost exclusively, stay in luxury suites, and even have taken amazing tours through Amazon jungles, world wonders, and more, paying for most of it in points and miles! I could go on and on about all this, but you can always check my Instagram @thekendraaraujo to see where we've been and how much it has really cost us!

In our house, we have a saying: "We will always do what we want." Even though it doesn't sound like much, it is the reality of how we live. The truth is, we apply this to anything and everything we decide, from dropping everything and leaving the country, to traveling the world for four months, to simply refusing to buy a house, to living in hotels in our hometown, even though people keep saying, "When are you guys going to settle down?" If I'm being completely honest, I have no idea what those words mean, but they sound to me like "wither and die."

Living life as a rebel is a decision.

Putting yourself first is a decision. I make—and struggle with— this decision every day. Every day, I choose not to let anyone else influence my aspirations in life—not my husband, not my mom, not my friends, and *certainly* not society's expectations.

This allows me to find my true passions in life—what really makes me happy to my core—and be grateful to be alive every single day. By having clear what those things are, I can plan for them, act on them, and be grateful for them every day. By doing this, I become a better person to everyone around me; I can be a better wife and a better teammate to my husband and a better daughter to my parents.

A happy fulfilled person will always be more helpful, be more inspirational, and—in the end—be less selfish than someone who struggles every day to put on a smile or to look at the bright side of life because he or she is too busy people-pleasing.

I decided to write this book because I know what it's like to be you—to be a young woman in a world where everybody wants to decide your future.

I know you know what you truly want in life. I have been through my own share of negative people, roadblocks, and even discouraging events that should've thrown me off my tracks.

Every time I heard a "You can't," "You shouldn't," "That is not possible," "That is not for you—you are a woman," I had the option either to agree with them, or follow my heart and find a way to make MY dreams a reality.

LIVING LIFE AS A REBEL IS A DECISION.

PUTTING YOURSELF FIRST IS A DECISION. I MAKE—AND STRUGGLE WITH—THIS DECISION EVERY DAY. EVERY DAY, I CHOOSE NOT TO LET ANYONE INFLUENCE MY ASPIRATIONS IN LIFE—NOT MY HUSBAND, NOT MY MOM, NOT MY FRIENDS, AND CERTAINLY NOT SOCIETY'S EXPECTATIONS.

You have power over your life. You have power over your decisions. It's time you accept that everything in your life is YOUR responsibility. You have one life. It's time for you to let go of everything and everyone that is putting you down and causing you to make decisions that don't really resonate with you and go after the things—and people—that do.

Your life's deepest desire could be to travel with no kids, like it is for me, or it could be owning a farm, growing your own food and selling at a farmer's market with your six children and husband helping you out, or it could be to make 7-figures in your corporate job and having a lover with no commitments, or it could be finally to stop caving in to what other people want and do what makes YOU happy.

YOU HAVE POWER OVER YOUR LIFE. YOU HAVE POWER OVER YOUR DECISIONS. IT'S TIME YOU ACCEPT THAT EVERYTHING IN YOUR LIFE IS YOUR RESPONSIBILITY. YOU HAVE ONE LIFE. IT'S TIME FOR YOU TO LET GO OF EVERYTHING AND EVERYONE THAT IS PUTTING YOU DOWN AND CAUSING YOU TO MAKE DECISIONS THAT DON'T REALLY RESONATE WITH YOU AND GO AFTER THE THINGS—AND PEOPLE—THAT DO.

NO JUDGMENT.

You can do those things. You can do anything you want. You just need to accept that you are worthy of your dreams and stop at nothing, for no-one, until you achieve them.

The coolest part is, you get to change what your dream life looks like whenever you feel like it because it's yours! Learn not to judge yourself and the world is yours.

LEARN NOT TO JUDGE YOURSELF AND THE WORLD IS YOURS.

In his book *The Front Row Factor*, Jon Vroman says, "Questions create focus, focus creates feelings, and feelings make up our emotional experience in life." All of us want our emotional experience to be the best at any given time, which is why we need to ask ourselves the deepest questions every day to make sure we are doing what is right for us.

Knowing what we want out of life is the first step toward getting it.

Answer these questions to yourself, being completely honest and without judging. If you think it helps, write down the answers.

What makes you happy to the point of feeling fully alive?

What are you doing right now that is only for you?

If you had one month to live, what would you do in your last 30 days?

Why wait for the last 30 days?

I challenge you to do one thing today that is only for you and that is in alignment with the things that make you come fully alive. Experience that feeling of complete joy and make that feeling a part of your daily routine starting right now. If you haven't yet, go to Chapter 16 in the Challenges section at the end of the book and start the 30-day challenge right now!

Yes, right now!

Don't wait until you are finished with this book. The life of your dreams awaits in the challenges. Why wait any longer? Start your first challenge immediately *and* continue reading from here. ;) See you on the other side!

WHAT MAKES YOU HAPPY TO THE POINT OF FEELING FULLY ALIVE?

EGYPT

TURKEY

CHAPTER 2

What's In It For You?

(or What is a Rebel Lifestyle and why would you want it?)

L et me start by explaining what a Rebel Lifestyle entails for me and what you can expect from living one. Then, I'll leave it up to you to decide what it means for you, because that is something ultra-personal that only you can answer. I'll explain...

I have been living life in the most rebellious ways for as long as I've known the difference. It's hard for me to describe what it is in a few words, but I will do my best in the next few paragraphs. I hope that this will give you an understanding of what you can accomplish by following the steps in this book.

The short and easy answer is that living a Rebel Lifestyle means to live life however you decide, wherever you want, and with whomever you please; letting go of what society, your family, or anyone else expects from you. Living *your* dream life.

Easy, huh?

I've come to realize that doing so is slightly more complicated than just *"doing you."*

It goes beyond deciding a career path, where to live, who to date, how many kids to have, or even what color to dye your hair.

YOUR true rebel lifestyle lies deep within you and it definitely is not the same as anybody else's.

Defining your own rebel lifestyle means diving inwards and discovering your true passions, desires, and dreams... the dreams and desires that may challenge the status quo, that may be beyond your comfort zone, but that are TRUE for you.

It means understanding what those are and transforming them into your reality against everyone and everything that gets in the way.

At the same time, it means knowing exactly who you are NOT: the things you are doing that don't really light you up but that you do because you are used to them or they are expected of you. It also is knowing exactly what (and who) you don't want in your life.

I am going to walk you through the steps to figure all of this out with each chapter, making sure you never feel lost or overwhelmed in the process. If you ever need extra support, or have further questions, feel free to join us in this fabulous community at *momisnotalwaysright.com/resources* where I and more rebel women are creating our very own rebel lifestyles.

Let's start with breaking all this down before we dive fully into it in the next chapter.

Being Honest with Yourself

We are programmed from the start, especially as women, to be "good girls," to pick up after ourselves, to offer help, to be somewhat modest, to have a sense of decency that men don't need to have on such a large scale.

All of these things, while they are meant to be "for our own good," play a big role in us automatically, almost unconsciously, burying our truest desires deep inside.

A quick example that you've probably heard before: if a guy sleeps around, he is considered a player, however, even though he may not the best candidate, you know that whenever he "decides" to settle down, he'll just do it. No problem.

If a girl has been sleeping around, however, she is labeled a slut (way worse than a player) and, "Poor guy who ends up with her; she's been everywhere."

That is a double standard in every book.

As women, we are taught either not to do that, or have learned to do it on the down low.

I'm not saying that either of these practices is wrong or right (no judgment, remember?). It's just a true, everyday, reminder of how we are told from the beginning of our lives to suppress our truest desires and to put on a face for the world portraying ourselves as perfect ladies.

The main issue with this is the guilt. I've experienced it in my own life for years and still struggle with it. The guilt trip that you go through every time you do what you aren't supposed to—you slept with a stranger, you ate that extra piece of cake, you said what was truly on your mind and someone got offended, even when you came home for Christmas without losing those extra pounds—can be suffocating.

The guilt that we've all felt is the main enemy of living life on your terms because it's such a powerful force. It can be self-induced or inflicted on us by society. It blinds us to our own wants and needs. More importantly, it denies us liberating self-acceptance.

To get a true hold of your life and make with it whatever you decide, you first need to grab that unwritten *Women's Guidelines* book that most of us have imprinted in our heads and flush it down the toilet.

GRAB THAT UNWRITTEN WOMEN'S GUIDELINES BOOK THAT MOST OF US HAVE IMPRINTED IN OUR HEADS AND FLUSH IT DOWN THE TOILET.

You can do anything you want—whatever that might be, whomever might be against it, and whatever it takes. You can accomplish it. To truly obtain it, you must first be honest with yourself about what that is.

If you answered the questions in the previous chapter, you may have a clearer idea what it is you want, however, now that the *Women's Guidelines* are forever gone, you now need to go deeper. Sit down with your thoughts and continue discovering what you truly want in your life, from the big things to the small things.

Consider:

- What are your true passions?
- What do you like in life?
- What do you dislike that you may be doing for someone else?
- What are your guilty pleasures?
- Why do they cause you to feel guilty?
- Who are you really?

Doing this powerful exercise will start to open your mind beyond what you thought acceptable to discover who you truly are. The key is to be completely honest with yourself. Do not judge what you are discovering as good, bad, or anything else. At this point, it is simply a discovery.

I've already shared part of the big things I want and do not want in life. Now let me tell you one of the small things I discovered after analyzing my wants.

I DON'T LIKE wearing a bra.

I simply don't.

It's oppressing. It's limiting. It could be considered sexist. I can never manage to keep the straps in place and strapless bras fall down even after I have the right size. I just don't like them. My bra is the first thing I take off every time I walk into my house.

I'm still wearing one because I love the push up look. I love how I look with fake-but-perfect boobs, so that's what's stopping me from taking it off completely while out. I don't judge the discoveries of not liking bras or of loving the look; I acknowledge them and accept them—which brings me to the next step: acceptance without judgment.

Accepting Who You are Inside and Out

Once you start digging into who you are, what you like, what you want, particularly what you don't like or want, it's time to ACCEPT that. Embrace your likes and wants. Understand that they are OK. You are allowed, and I'm encouraging you, to liberate yourself from judgment and accept who you truly are on the inside. Your ideas are OK. What you want is OK. Your dreams and hopes are OK. Your desired behavior is OK.

You are not meant to live a life of GUILT. Accepting yourself is the first step toward releasing that guilt and turning it into true acceptance. Not only accepting that your likes and wants are OK, but rather that you are WORTHY of everything that you want.

There is another key aspect to acceptance. It's not just your inner self that you need to accept, but also your shell. One of the main roadblocks in the path of living life on our own terms is the lack of confidence we may have in ourselves.

This insecurity starts with our bodies. We'll dig deeper into this in the next chapters, however, it's important that you realize right now that you only have one body—just like you only have one life and one mind.

YOU ARE ALLOWED, AND I'M ENCOURAGING YOU, TO LIBERATE YOURSELF FROM JUDGMENT AND ACCEPT WHO YOU TRULY ARE ON THE INSIDE.

If you don't accept yourself entirely, you won't be able to accomplish your biggest dreams because you'll always be fighting with yourself. Worst of all, you'll leave that door open for others to attack you, to bring you down, and to push you out of the path of true happiness.

Why? Because if you don't accept who you are on the outside, every time someone criticizes you, you are allowing those words to hurt; not because someone said them, but because deep inside, you believe them to be true.

Let that sink in.

No one can hurt you unless you give them permission. Accept who you are in every aspect and you'll be bulletproof. Let go of the belief that you NEED to be different, "I have to lose weight for summer," "My legs are pale. I need to get tanned to look right," or "My hair is never right" mentality. You are perfect and you deserve love. Truly accepting yourself inside and out is a main ingredient to reaching all of your goals.

YOU ARE PERFECT AND YOU DESERVE LOVE. TRULY ACCEPTING YOURSELF INSIDE AND OUT IS A MAIN INGREDIENT TO REACHING ALL OF YOUR GOALS.

You may be wondering at this point, "Hey, you just said you like the look of fake boobs! What's up with that?" Let me tell you, I SAID EXACTLY THE SAME THING, at first. I was thinking, "What is all that about? Here I am trying to tell other women to accept their bodies and I myself like the way my boobs look only when wearing a bra, possibly on account of this vain idea of perfect boobs."

Then it hit me.

ACCEPTING YOURSELF IS NOT IN CONFLICT WITH WANTING TO IMPROVE YOURSELF. IT ONLY MEANS THAT YOU DO IT OUT OF A PLACE OF LOVE INSTEAD A PLACE OF HATE.

I was judging myself. I was judging my thoughts. I was judging my wants. I was assuming what would others think of me. Judgment is your worst enemy, especially self-judgment, because the whole point of acceptance is all-encompassing.

First of all, you DON'T read minds, so don't assume what other people will think; it shouldn't matter anyway. Second, you can't pick and choose what you judge and what you don't. I like how fake boobs look and there is nothing wrong with that.

How does that fall into the whole body-acceptance situation? Let me explain...

Fair warning: I'm going to totally butcher the next part here since the girls that lead the Body Positivity community say it way better, however, here is the main point:

Accepting yourself is not in conflict with wanting to improve yourself. It only means that you do it out of a place of love instead a place of hate.

Read that again.

If you feel the need, work on improving yourself from a place of love instead of doing it from a place of hate. Here is a common example:

January 1st is here and you say to yourself, "This year I'm going to lose 10 pounds because these huge thighs are beyond disgusting! I can't even wear short skirts anymore. I hate them and the cellulite! AGH! I need to lose that extra weight to make this less embarrassing for spring."

We've all been there and it SUCKS.

Try saying this to yourself: "This year I'm going feed my body with all the nutrients it needs to perform at its peak while also cutting down on junk food since I've been consuming it a lot. Studies show how toxic junk food can be for my health and overall performance. My body never stops working for me and it's time I give it what it needs to thrive."

See the difference?

The result may end up being the same 10 pounds off or not, however, in the first example you are setting yourself up for failure by setting this goal as a punishment to yourself for "not looking perfect" (perfect according to whom?) versus deciding you are going to improve your overall health by making smarter decisions on your food intake out of appreciation to your body. You will feel happy with your actions and you will stay motivated for far longer, maybe even permanently, because you'll love how you feel inside and out!

I have struggled.

It has taken me years and countless hours of reading and meditation to get to the point of accepting my body as it is. To truly accept my body and to love it has been a major challenge and turning point in my life.

I still struggle. It's a never-ending work.

Liking the way my boobs look in a bra is not against everything I've accomplished since I don't hate my boobs for being too small like I did in my teenage days. On the contrary, I love and appreciate them now and I want them to be free all the time instead of being squeezed into a bra. I also love how they look when I'm wearing a bra. Right now, I am opting for giving in to

TO TRULY BE ABLE TO WAKE UP EVERY DAY, ADMIRE YOURSELF SO MUCH INSIDE AND OUT THAT YOU AUTOMATICALLY THINK, "F WHOMEVER DOESN'T LIKE WHAT I'M ABOUT TO DO BECAUSE I'M ABOUT TO CONQUER THE WORLD. JUST WATCH ME," AND MEAN IT, YOU HAVE TO LOVE YOURSELF.

this look I love. This is simply where I am in my own journey and there is nothing wrong with that. Hear that again.

There is nothing wrong with my wants, just like there is nothing wrong with yours. Accepting this is key. Loving your overall self is far more important.

This brings us to our next step toward living your own rebel dream life...

Love Who You Are

"In a society that profits from your self doubt, liking yourself is a rebellious act" - Caroline Caldwell.

Accept that the way your mind works is totally perfect and that the thoughts that come out of it are worth exploring. Understand that whatever you want out of life is attainable if you are willing to put in the work. Let's not forget, accepting your body as your one and only and cherishing it every day is a major step towards your dream life. Living a rebel lifestyle, however, means going further than just acceptance.

To truly be able to wake up every day, admire yourself so much inside and out that you automatically think, "F whomever doesn't like what I'm about to do because I'm about to conquer the world. Just watch me," and mean it, you have to LOVE yourself.

Love yourself so much that there is no stopping you. No one and nothing can get in the way of you achieving your goals because you come first. You become your biggest love story.

Think about the person you love the most.

If you didn't think of yourself, do it again. You. You should be the person you love the most. I'm not saying you are meant to love everyone else less than you do, but you should love yourself more than you love anyone else and you should be above everyone else in your priorities list.

Other people will come and go, whoever they are, but You have been with You since the start and will be until the end. You will have to face yourself every morning, every night, and every moment in between.

You have the power to love the person who is looking back at you in the mirror, to be proud of you, to encourage you, and to motivate you, or to be ashamed of you, maybe even hiding, or, what's worse—indifferent.

True freedom is being able to look yourself in the eye and say, "I've got this," and mean it. The moment you truly become your own biggest fan, there will be no stopping you. Try it!

Choose to Spend Your Time and Money as You Want

People have this need to tell you how you are spending your money wrong. Unless wrong means spending money when something could be free, I don't understand this reason. In all honesty, I can't say I haven't done it myself, however, why the need?

People are entitled to spend their money as they see fit, especially if it's in ways that truly make them happy and won't jeopardize the roof over their heads. Living a rebel lifestyle means being able to let go of any guilt, any self-imposed judgment or social expectation, and deciding what you want to do with your free time, with your cash and, ultimately, with your life.

LIVING A REBEL LIFESTYLE MEANS BEING ABLE TO LET GO OF ANY GUILT, ANY SELF-IMPOSED JUDGMENT OR SOCIAL EXPECTATION, AND DECIDING WHAT YOU WANT TO DO WITH YOUR FREE TIME, WITH YOUR CASH AND, ULTIMATELY, WITH YOUR LIFE.

I'm not saying that you should just quit on your debt because "you don't want to pay them anymore." If you are in debt, or are considering a large purchase, it should be because you decided for yourself, while analyzing the pros and cons, that it was for your OWN good, it was going to bring YOU happiness, that you could afford it, and most importantly, that it's not to try to meet some socially accepted status quo or anything else.

From going to the movies on your own to attending a certain concert, or flying to Hawaii for New Year's, or even buying that cute pair of shoes that will "take three months to pay off, but that are absolutely worth it." Maybe the wiser decision would be to save up for the shoes instead of getting into debt over them. This might mean limiting yourself to only two drinks at girls-night-out. Even still, you shouldn't let anyone put you down for your wants. Your true friends should understand that this is something you are doing for yourself and should support you. Only you can decide what really matters to you with your time and with your money.

As of today, I have been married for four and half years. During all this time, we've been asked constantly, by almost everyone around us:

"When are you going to buy a house? When are you going to have kids? Why do you party so much? Why do you spend so much money on traveling (if they only knew...ha ha) instead of putting it aside for a home? Why don't you have stable jobs that allow you to save for retirement?"

These are clear examples of well-meaning people trying to tell us what to do with our lives.

I wouldn't change any trip we've ever taken, any Friday night drinks that turned into Saturday morning, or any cozy night in taking in the view of our rented condo, for a massive debt from a house I don't really like, or a 9 – 5 job that wouldn't allow me to take 5 days off on a whim to go climb Machu Picchu. It's called *priorities* and we have clearly stated ours.

The truth is, most people don't know your daily routines, your spending and saving habits, your true dreams and goals. What's worse is that most of them don't want to know. Most people are not really interested in you fulfilling your dreams.

They are not even interested in fulfilling their own dreams.

They wouldn't know what their perfect lives would look like if they hit them in the face because they've never asked themselves the questions. They've never questioned the status quo. They've never questioned their future. What's worse is that they've never questioned themselves.

Sacrificing your life for someone else's ideals wouldn't make you or anyone else happy. It would only satisfy some elusive ideal that might not even be real to begin with. You can't really live your life to please others—it's been proven time and time again that this doesn't work and never has. Letting other people decide for you would mean signing your life away over what people might say. That, my rebel friend, is the biggest enemy of success.

Now answer the question, "What does *your* dream life really look like?"

Choose to Spend Your Time Only with those Who Respect and Cherish You

We are social beings. We are not meant to be on our own, isolated, living as hermits. Some people may be able to pull that off, but the other 99.99% of us depend on other people for a lot of things, including food. I mean, I don't go out to some little cute farm 40 minutes outside of the city and make butter on my own. I find it perfectly cold waiting for me in the grass-fed department.

In this same sense, we depend on other people to bounce ideas off of, to go out, to have a great time, to share what's in our minds, or on our hearts. We also need an amazing lover. If all these people are the same person: WIN-WIN!

We need a tribe: a tribe of people who actually like us and will be in our corner through good and bad—especially in the bad when it's time to let us know we are taking the wrong way.

You have a limited amount of time on this planet. You are free, or should be free, to spend it with whomever you feel DESERVES it because that is the one thing you can never take back.

Take a moment to look back at this past month. Who have you spent the most of your time with? When were you your best you? When did you have the most fun? Who were you with? When did you feel attacked or pushed down? Why were you in that situation surrounded by those people?

Time is so valuable that you need to take a step back and realize who are the true winners in your life. Who are the friends that bring out the best in you, who truly care for you—inside and out, who don't put you down to make themselves look better, the ones who respect your dreams—even if they don't understand them, as well as your personality?

The same thing goes with lovers. Make sure you are choosing to be intimate with someone who shows respect for you, who cherishes the time you give, your ideas, your dreams, your bad moods, your body, and everything else you are sharing.

These same things apply to your family members. Are they your biggest supporters or your loudest critics?

TO BE WHO YOU TRULY ARE, AND LIVE THE LIFE YOU WANT, YOU NEED TO MAKE SURE THAT YOU ARE SURROUNDING YOURSELF WITH PEOPLE WHO WILL PUSH YOU TO GET THERE.

It is commonly said that you are the combination of the five people you spend the most of your time with. To be who you truly are, and live the life you want, you need to make sure that you are surrounding yourself with people who will push you to get there. Make a real analysis of who embodies those characteristics and who doesn't; it may be time to cut them loose.

You can't afford to waste your precious time with people who don't appreciate it. Like the Mexican saying goes, "Mas vale sola que mal acompañada" (Better to be alone than in bad company).

Actually, it's not just in your physical community where you can find your biggest supporters. Hello! We live in the age of technology! From Facebook groups to Instagram communities, never underestimate the power that a supportive online tribe can bring!

I have changed my life thanks these supportive communities and I'll show you exactly how to accomplish this in the next chapters. You can start to make the same analysis of your social media "friends" like you are doing for your real-life friends.

One last thing to keep in mind: friendship is a two-way street.

You need to be the best supporter of your friends, lovers, and family to help them achieve their dreams. Believe in them even when they don't believe in themselves—even if you don't agree with their goals (remember not to judge).

Only then can you expect the same in return.

Defend Yourself Against ANYONE Who Gets in the Way of Your Dreams

For you truly to accomplish everything you desire for yourself, you will have to become your own cheerleader. Armed with the amazing love you'll have for yourself and the incredible support you'll find in your tribe backing you up, you are going to go out into the world.

You'll encounter thousands of opinions, ideas, and dream-killers who will come at you and you will face them with the determination of 1,000 women before you. You'll push through and not let a simple, "No," "You can't," "It's impossible," "You are just a woman," or "You'll never make it," bring you down.

You'll know that nothing is impossible. Nothing is too hard for you. You CAN achieve anything you've ever dreamed of. You also understand that it will take a lot of work—work that you'll do because you really have no other option.

It's either go after your dreams or the non-option of sitting down looking out the window watching others succeed while you wither and die as you criticize them since odds are you'll become one of the haters.

I would love to say it's easy, but you already know it's not.

I can say with incredible certainty that the more you find that inner love for yourself, the easier each battle will get. You'll be able to brush off the haters and continue working on your goals. With time, it will become second nature to you to recognize quickly the negative vibes someone is sending you and to walk away not-so-slowly because you don't need that in your life.

Unfortunately, these are not just strangers. Sometimes they are in your house, in your group of friends, even disguised as part of your team—they are the hardest ones to recognize and to fight.

You were not put in this world to explain yourself to others. No one is walking around explaining their goals to everyone and then defending them with all who disagree. Why should you? What's more important, why should you keep telling your dreams to those who won't support them?

Let me give you a real-life example from my experience.

While deciding to write this book—and while writing it—I wanted to get some accountability. At first, I thought it good to let everyone know that I was working on this long overdue project of mine so I would be inclined to finish it.

Then I started to notice the reactions.

Some people laughed like, "What are you even writing a book about?" Others were seriously curious about what was it about.

My cousin, who is one of my best friends, was the one person not to ask, but to say, "That is incredible! I can't wait to read it!"

Every time we saw each other afterward or texted, she would always ask, "How is the book coming? What chapter are you on now? When can I tell everyone that you are a published author?" She was truly interested in making me fulfill my goal because she truly believed in me and in my mission and she kept me accountable.

I can say with a hand on my heart that fear of setting a bad example for her, and disappointing her, or worse, my "quitting" resulting in her not following through with her own dreams, are some of the reasons this book saw the light of day (against all of my own self-imposed insecurities).

This is the kind of person you want in your tribe.

Treat your dreams like you treat your hoo-ha and only share them with those that will appreciate them and give you nothing but love to accomplish them. The rest of the people may not want to see you succeed. What is the point of trying to convince someone who doesn't want to be convinced?

Live your life. Tighten your group. Let those who don't fit slowly fade away. It's a life or death situation here.

Finally...

Let Go

Letting go is the next logical step after you learn to accept, appreciate, and love yourself. Learn to identify what you want to do with your time and money. Identify who is worthy of your time and money. Recognize who is truly in your tribe.

Letting go means stripping yourself from the ideas that have held you back. From the insecurities that you have created for yourself or have been taught to believe to the daily judgments that you make against yourself, and others, to every single thought that you have that is some sort of self-sabotage for not going after what you want.

The minute you realize you are saying, or are about to say, something negative about yourself, stop it! Say something positive instead.

Letting go also means distancing yourself from the situations that put you in the wrong mindset or that you are only doing to satisfy someone else. Is gossiping a huge thing with your coworkers? Is girls' night turning into trashing-everyone-and-everything around you? Are extended family reunions a constant reminder of "how fat you've gotten," or "when are you getting married?" How about going to the gym only because you are punishing your body? If so, it may be time to let those practices go.

I'm not saying you should stop exercising, or not go out anymore, or not go see your family. If they are becoming negative situations for you, however, you may want to rethink how you are approaching them.

Change your routine to something that will make you feel good about yourself. Maybe running is a way of being alone with your thoughts and re-centering yourself. What about on girls' night, suggesting different activities that change everyone's mindset?

At family reunions, maybe make a quick stop of hi and bye or avoid conversations with those who bring you down—focus on your true teammates. I'll give you plenty of examples on how to improve these in another chapter, but keep in mind that the effort should be worth it.

If the people in those situations are not the right people for you, then any action to improve them might be wasted and it might drain you for nothing. Think of the people and then take a look at the moment.

Letting go means cutting loose the haters. You don't need them in your life, especially at the beginning when you are still strengthening your self-love muscles and are more susceptible to aggressions. This requires a deep dive into your own heart because deep down you know who belongs and who doesn't.

Letting go is simply setting yourself up for success by surrounding yourself with the people, the events, and the support you'll need while walking the path of self-discovery and of achieving the life of your dreams.

Your own rebel lifestyle is not a destination you'll get to at the end of this book. It's a discovery that you'll make each day with every page you read and onwards. You will learn to put yourself first every day from now on. You'll create your personal, true, and unique way of life from deep within you.

The biggest misconception of living *the life of your dreams* is that you need to "go and get it." Yes, some of our dreams require lots of money and time and you do have to work for that; however, your true dream life—your rebel lifestyle—is something that you create every day in every situation with everyone.

It starts by being 100% honest with yourself in your thoughts, your words, and your actions, by loving yourself so much that you won't take the smallest degree of bullshit from anyone— especially from a supposed group of friends or a lover.

It continues by showing respect for others and demanding the same for yourself, by not judging, by spending your time however you see fit with those who value it, and by letting go of any negative thoughts, people, and situations that are not challenges to make you grow, but instead are haters who want to see you fail.

Now, take action!

Now that you know the basics to start living the life you want, open to the Challenges section and start the first challenge NOW! If you started it already, KEEP GOING!

Instead of waiting until the end to take action, take advantage of this momentum and start right away! Keep reading the book as part of your challenge and take a leap forward for yourself!

PERU

PERU

REBEL LIFESTYLE DESIGN STEP 1

UNCONDITIONAL SELF LOVE

CHAPTER 3

Accepting Your Inner Self

B y now, you know that in order to start living life on your terms, to become a full rebel, you must first define those terms. You must understand your true passions in every aspect of your life, accept them as your true self, and turn them into goals while falling in love with yourself.

Now, start actually defining those passions—the things that make you get out of bed every morning, the things that make you smile all the way to your heart. Also, discover the things that are in the way of you taking action on those goals.

If you truly are committed to making this change, the very first roadblock that we will tackle is the way you approach your daily actions, your long-term dreams, your ideas, and your life goals.

From now on, you will be BRUTALLY honest with yourself about everything that you do in order to identify three things:

1. The actions you take for you.
2. The actions you take for others.
3. The actions you take in spite of you.

That last one is the most important one to uncover and conquer. You must conquer your mind to conquer your future.

My mom and aunts like to tell this *funny* story of when I was about 4 or 5 years old and we were at Toys Я Us picking up Christmas presents. According to the story, I approached my mom and said, "Mom, I want a [toy] gun." She responded, "What? Why do you want a gun?" "I want to kill my brother." (He is one year older than me and I'm pretty sure he had a gun and was "killing" me while playing.) "But Kendra, you are girl!" Deciding not to give up yet on my request, I replied unsuccessfully, "OK, Mom. How about a pink gun?" They started laughing.

Our ideas and, therefore, our dreams as women have been shut down by society from the beginning of our lives: from picking up a toy that's "wrong" on account of our gender to choosing the "wrong" marital status. This has made uncovering our ideal life goals a harder task than it should be. I was taught that if it's pink, it's OK to want it and that if it's violent, it's a boy's toy. This is only scratching the surface.

Now, how about what you want that has been buried so deep inside you that you don't even know if you want it anymore? Or even if you should...What have you wanted that you've been told is wrong because of your sex, social status, skin color, background, or worse, it's wrong because of status quo?

Answer the following questions with a hand on your heart, maybe even closing your eyes to visualize the answer, and very importantly, being BRUTALLY honest with yourself. Remember NO JUDGMENT. Let every idea that comes to you flow and answer the questions:

- If you could do anything in your life knowing that you couldn't fail and no one would judge you, what would do?
- If you could be anything you wanted, again no failure and no outside judgment, what would you be?
- Imagine you have a magic lamp and you could change anything in your life within a year. What would your life look like a year from now? (Note: things that are not in your control, such as "Bringing Fido back from dog heaven" are not accurate answers.)

Write your answers in a journal or even in the "notes" app of your phone and add the date to help you have a record of what you deeply desire at this point in your life.

Take a hard look at the things you wrote and discover how you feel when reading them out loud.

- Do you feel they're ridiculous?
- Do you believe it's possible to achieve these goals?
- Do you think it's impossible to attain even one of those things?
- Do you see them as a clear path into your future that you've always known? Like your true self has finally emerged and it can be your reality from now on?
- Remember—brutal honesty. Write next to them what your TRUE thoughts are.

Take Responsibility

With a clearer idea of where your thoughts drift when you give them permission, you now have a better understanding of where your true terms reside. Knowing, or starting to understand, what these dreams and goals are is only the beginning. It is only the first step to turning your life into one you love.

What if, instead of daydreaming, and future-gazing, I asked you to look at your present?

- What does your present look like?
- Is it at all resembling what you aspire for yourself?

- Are you the person you want to be?
- Is your day-to-day situation your ideal scenario?

Odds are that you are reading this book because it might not be. Maybe it's getting there and you just want to improve yourself. Whatever your situation, there will be no major breakthrough without you accepting responsibility for where you are.

You are where you are because you decided to be.

Repeat that.

YOU ARE WHERE YOU ARE BECAUSE YOU DECIDED TO BE.

REPEAT THAT.

YOU ARE WHERE YOU ARE BECAUSE YOU CHOSE TO BE.

You are where you are because you CHOSE to be.

You chose to do what you are doing each day. You chose to wear what you are wearing and to eat what you are eating, to chase your dreams or not to chase them, because you can also choose by omission. What's even more important to understand is that you choose to feel the way you do about everything that happens in your life.

You might say, "I didn't choose this life. It happened to me!" Well, I'm sorry, but if you were dealt a "bad hand" and you are still in the gutter, it's because you haven't made your mind up to get out of there. That is the cold hard truth. Don't believe me? Ask Jeff Hoffman, inventor of Priceline and the self-check-in machines at airports.

Jeff was born in a poor family in a small town where no one had any aspirations. He, however, most definitely didn't assume the victim role. He got himself into Harvard against every single person he knew, family included, with no trust fund—or anyone to support him, for that matter—and went on to become a serial entrepreneur, philanthropist, and multi-millionaire.

No, you are not a victim. If your story is way worse than Jeff's and you are still taking on the "victim" role, take a hard look. With brutal honesty, ask yourself why.

- Why are things the same?
- Why isn't my life getting better?
- Why am I still in this awful situation?

If you believe it is because of someone else, take another guess.

Take full responsibility for your life and everything in it. Take control of your life. Decide for yourself what you want, what you don't want, and what tomorrow will look like.

Are you in a crappy job? Leave.

No savings? Stop the daily Starbucks, put that money in the bank, search for a better career situation, and quit.

Are you in a crappy relationship? LEAVE. No excuses.

Do you have nowhere to go? Stay with a friend, coworker, or in an AirBnB for a while.

Are your friends not supportive of your dreams? Find a new tribe.

You have the power to make your life whatever you want it to be in spite of where you are right now. There are huge steps you can take. There are small ones, too. The most important thing is that you understand that you come first and that you do everything in your power every single day to make yourself happy, complete, and fulfilled.

YOU HAVE THE POWER TO MAKE YOUR LIFE WHATEVER YOU WANT IT TO BE IN SPITE OF WHERE YOU ARE RIGHT NOW. THERE ARE HUGE STEPS YOU CAN TAKE. THERE ARE SMALL ONES, TOO. THE MOST IMPORTANT THING IS THAT YOU UNDERSTAND THAT YOU COME FIRST AND THAT YOU DO EVERYTHING IN YOUR POWER EVERY SINGLE DAY TO MAKE YOURSELF HAPPY, COMPLETE, AND FULFILLED.

Don't worry. These harder decisions may look scary at this point, however, I promise you that when you are done with all the exercises in this book, these big life-changing decisions will not only become easier to take, but you'll embrace them as the next—and only—logical step into living the life of your dreams.

Embrace Your Truth

Now that you accept that you are solely responsible for where you are in your life and you have a clearer idea of where you want to be, the next step, as all you smart ladies already know, is acceptance.

To accept who you truly are is easier said than done. Most of us have been taught that our ambitions are wrong if they don't agree with society's expectations. They are either too small, "too out there," or worse, too big and too life-altering to be acceptable. How sad is that?

How sad is it that our society, including sometimes family members and so-called friends, would rather see us unhappy following the "normal" guidelines instead of seeing us thrive chasing our dreams only because it challenges what they believe?

A lot of us have it easy. We can study, work, and even sleep with whomever we want to; we will be judged for it, but at

ACCEPT WHAT YOU WANT FOR YOURSELF, WHAT YOU WANT IN THIS LIFE, AND YOUR ASPIRATIONS. LET ABSOLUTELY NO-ONE TELL YOU THAT YOUR ASPIRATIONS AND DESIRES ARE NOT GOOD—NOT EVEN YOUR MOM.

least we CAN do it. There are other women in situations where it's literally impossible for them to do that. Think tribe-women that, to this day, get their genitals cut off or mutilated as part of some ritual. We are lucky. I feel incredibly grateful for being able to write this book and hope you feel just as grateful to be able to read it as a free person.

Let's take all that self-doubt and self-judgment and flush it down the toilet because we owe it to all those girls to be the best we can possibly be. Maybe by making our lives the best we can, we can empower the women around us to do it, too, and hopefully create a ripple effect that will eventually reach those places on earth where these words are badly needed.

Believe in yourself.

Believe that you have the power to make your life your own.

Accept what you want for yourself, what you want in this life, and your aspirations. Let absolutely no-one tell you that your aspirations and desires are not good—not even your mom.

Accept that you will not be cheered on by everyone you know as you travel the path of achieving your dreams. There will be haters. There will be doubters. There will be people who will actively try to make you fail. It won't be your job to fight them, but it will be your job to choose NOT to believe what they say.

Stay away from them whenever possible. Find support within yourself and your tribe.

You will need to work on yourself first, which is why I'm breaking down this book into sections before the challenges. You will need your foundations to be incredibly steady to face the outside world in Section 2.

We will build your confidence from the inside out so when the time comes for you to face the doubters, you will have no need even to hear them. You'll know you are on the right track. Haters mean you are doing something right that is scaring other people.

Now go back to the answers you wrote at the beginning of this chapter. Read them out loud once again. If you feel like they are ridiculous, read them again. This time, try to visualize yourself actually living that life. See yourself a year from now living the situation you described in question 3. Go further than that and look deep into your future. See yourself being the person you wish to be, doing the things that make you happy in whatever scenario that might be. Close this book, set a timer for 5 minutes, and visualize your perfect life.

It's OK if you want to change your initial answer. It's OK if you don't know yet how to accomplish those dreams. We'll get to that in Section 2. Right now, you need to believe you can be that person, do those things, and have that life.

If this visualization makes you smile and truly happy—just by thinking about it—it's your heart speaking to you telling you what you truly want. Accept it.

Believe it can happen and ACCEPT these wants as your true self. This is what your inner self desires. Whatever it might be, IT'S OK TO WANT IT. Write down what a day in your perfect life would look like. Every day, visualize yourself already living it. This will keep you on track to achieving it and will remind you every day to take the necessary steps to get there.

It's completely OK if, at first, you feel like you are faking it. Deep inside, you might say "this is all good, but honestly I don't see this happening." Even then, especially then, do it. Every day. In an upcoming chapter, I'll go deeper into how to talk to yourself when you are just not feeling the positivity—without faking it and without lying to yourself—in a way that feels genuine and true.

Right now, work on repeating your visualization every day. See yourself already living it until you believe it in your heart—until there is absolutely no doubt that these will be you in reality. What you need to understand is that YOU ARE that person.

Deep inside you, that is your true self and those are your true aspirations. Accept that without judging them. See them. Manifest them into your life. Start living them.

This is what I visualize everyday:

"I wake up in a hotel suite we didn't have to pay for somewhere in the world. Yahir is next to me still sleeping. I go to the living area do my "Miracle Morning" practice. I can finally do a headstand on my own during yoga time. Next, I take 5 minutes to list what I want for my day as part of the "Magic Money" philosophy. I then go back to bed. We order room service for breakfast, open up our computers to work for around one hour in bed which provides enough every day to support our lifestyle. I'm focusing my work on empowering women to live the lives of their dreams and to achieve their goals while I'm living mine. I feel completely fulfilled from my work and have an incredible outsourced support team. We then close our laptops, finish breakfast, and go explore what this new city has to offer. We walk around. We sight-see. Then, we meet up with some friends: new ones or some who traveled with us—maybe it's family. We find a cool local bar and finish up the day with dinner and drinks in between laughs. When I put my head on my pillow, I feel incredibly grateful for the life I'm living and think, 'What A RIDE!'"

I then visualize further.

"We are at the airport heading back home in first class seats that— again—we didn't have to pay for with unlimited champagne on the flight ;). A limo picks us up, takes us to our oceanfront home with glass walls, a pool and a "Mah Jong" sofa from Roche Bobois (best sofa ever). We meet our friends and family to catch up and have a great time. We feel incredibly grateful to have them in our lives. We know they are our true tribe and that we support each other in our goals and dreams. Again, my head in bed, I say once more, 'What a ride!' while I'm thinking where to go next. I know that we already have the points for our next trip."

This is *my* unique daily visualization. I repeat it to myself every day. As of the time of writing this book, I've had that day become 90% reality on more than one occasion within the past month. For example, we were in Venice, had a complimentary suite upgrade, and ended up sipping champagne on a gondola! (I still can't do that headstand, though. That is harder than I thought!) That is what *I* want. These are my UNIQUE terms for MY life.

This last Christmas, and my following birthday celebration in January, my mom made a point of telling everyone that she wanted a grandchild from us and for us to finally have a house of our own because "we are not getting any younger."

Talk about peer-pressure in front of the whole family and friends!!

It's not that she doesn't want me to be happy; the reality is that she can't see that I'm not the person that is going to follow all the rules in life. To go from college graduate to married – steady job – kids – house – dog – smile at family pictures, is simply not me.

I don't have her knowledge. As hard as I try to understand that she truly believes that she is doing it for my own good and out of her motherly love, I know that it all comes down to society's expectations. One of the biggest lessons I had to learn in order not to let my mom's loving advice interfere with my own pursuit of happiness is that it has nothing to do with me.

When I was 19 or 20 years old, my mom told me that if I got good grades in college, she would pay for my nose job. WHAT! I didn't want a nose job. I've never wanted a nose job. I am more than perfectly happy with my nose. It's perfect for my face and for me.

I've never ever felt like it needed an "upgrade;" however, somehow, she thought that I may need a nose job and she was happily offering to pay for it so I wouldn't feel self-conscious about it. That was the first time that I got it: she was doing it out of love, but she was doing it because that is how SHE felt.

Maybe when she was younger, she felt she didn't look good enough and wished someone would have offered that to her or to have the means herself to correct it. I wish I could go back in time and tell that teenager or young adult woman, "You are the most beautiful woman ever. You don't need to change a thing. You are a QUEEN as you are."

She has deep-rooted insecurities which I believe stem from the fact that she has four sisters and an old-school, loving-but-judgmental, mother. I'm sure they spent all day calling each other fat if someone ate a donut.

When someone, anyone, tries to tell you what you are supposed to do, it says more about the critic than it does about you. Unfortunately, sometimes is hard to distinguish the good advice from the bad and it's easy to let others' judgments bring you down, make you doubt your dreams, or worse—doubt yourself.

I know exactly how that feels. I've had induced insecurities that I had never noticed until someone pointed them out as wrong. For example, I tend to laugh "too hard," or I am "ultra-selfish" for not wanting kids...

I know now that I have the power to look beyond that. Most importantly, I have the power to do with my life whatever I PLEASE. I can do anything I want... and so can you.

We all can live the lives of our dreams. We all can be happy. We all can support each other. That is why the no-judgment rule is so important in our community. So is our brutal honesty with ourselves.

Take a good, hard look at your everyday activities. Figure out what you are doing every day to make yourself happy, achieve your goals, and what you are doing for someone else in spite of you.

CREATE YOUR OWN VISUALIZATION OF WHAT A PERFECT DAY LOOKS LIKE TO YOU. FIGURE OUT WHAT IT IS THAT TRULY MAKES YOUR HEART JUMP WITH JOY, IN SPITE OF WHAT EVERYONE ELSE THINKS. THEN, WORK EACH DAY TO MAKE IT A REALITY.

I don't mean when you are doing a favor for a friend—always do those if they're within your means. I mean when you get married to your less-than-perfect boyfriend because you are turning 30 and "this is it, time's up."

When you pass up on dessert at a family reunion because everyone will start to comment on the extra pounds you put on this year. When you don't dye your hair pink because you are a "serious professional" now even though it's what you've always wanted.

Create your own visualization of what a perfect day looks like to you. Figure out what it is that truly makes your heart jump with joy, in spite of what everyone else thinks. Then, work each day to make it a reality.

Make everyday small decisions that will get you there. Once you are mindful of what you are doing each day, you'll see the little actions that are either pushing you closer to your dreams or pulling you farther away. Start with those small actions and you will get there!

Remember, everything that you want for your life is absolutely and unequivocally RIGHT.

Even if your mom doesn't get it. Even if it doesn't follow the norm. Even if you are the only one who can see it.

It's PERFECT!

You CAN have it. Embrace it. Embrace YOURSELF—just as you ARE.

How do you go from uncovering your true aspirations to believing they are possible and actually following through with them?

One day at a time.

Today you read this chapter. Tomorrow you'll read the next. Then you'll do the workbook and start following through with the 30-day challenge... and it will all happen one day at a time until one day, you realize you are living life on your own terms and will feel so grateful and joyful for it.

VENICE

VENICE

CHAPTER 4

Accepting Your Outer Self

ast time I checked my iPhone, I had about 23,000 pictures on my photos app and about 10,000 more from the GoPro memory chip. Even though these pictures were taken during our trips around the world in some of the most beautiful places ever, and also from everyday life, fewer than 500 pictures have been posted on social media.

I don't believe every single picture you take should be posted, however, it is important to acknowledge the reason you're not posting them. For example, when you are experiencing something so awesome like a couple of years ago when we were walking on the Great Wall of China, that is something you want to post about.

If you were to search the hashtag #greatwallofchina, you would find the most wonderful out-of-this-world pictures of magazine-worthy people with the most amazing editing and perfect background in the perfect spot, with their amazing body and just perfect expression with millions of likes.

Well that didn't happen to me.

I mean I was in the right place—*world wonder, Hello!* with the right company, however, it took nearly 50 pictures to get one that I liked and that I considered looked "acceptable" for social media.

WHAT A LOAD OF CRAP!

I was hating on myself.

I hated the way I looked. I felt ugly for not having make up on. My short hair wasn't helping. I felt fat for eating "badly" for the past month while traveling. I dressed to hide myself. I felt awful for wearing the wrong outfit. I was wearing the wrong shoes.

On top of that, I was feeling like the worst person on earth for having these feelings when I was supposed to just be happy enjoying!! Why wasn't I just happy?!?! This made me feel even worse.

All I wanted was an out-of-a-magazine perfect picture so I could post it on Instagram and Facebook and impress everyone. I was in a downward spiral that made it impossible for me to take a "good" picture, or to even like the way I looked. Worst of all, I was dragging my husband with me.

This mental trick that we play on ourselves is the most damaging thing we can do to ourselves, our self-esteem, and ultimately our lives. We self-sabotage our own efforts to live the lives of our dreams by hating on our bodies and comparing ourselves to others. Unfortunately, this is a practice that most of us engage in on a daily basis.

> THIS MENTAL TRICK THAT WE PLAY ON OURSELVES IS THE MOST DAMAGING THING WE CAN DO TO OURSELVES, OUR SELF-ESTEEM, AND ULTIMATELY OUR LIVES. WE SELF-SABOTAGE OUR OWN EFFORTS TO LIVE THE LIVES OF OUR DREAMS BY HATING ON OUR BODIES AND COMPARING OURSELVES TO OTHERS.

At this point, you have worked so hard to accept what you want out of life, to accept that your dreams and ideas are completely OK and achievable, and you've started to feel that invincible feeling that comes with the realization that as soon as you accept who you truly are on the inside, no one can stop you.

This same lesson goes hand in hand with your outer self.

Our bodies are just as perfect and as correct as our ideas and dreams are. They are not wrong, ugly, or in need of change to be accepted. They are perfect, beautiful, and deserve all of our love.

You will learn to fall so deeply in love with yourself that no one will ever be able to point a finger at you and make you tremble because you'll know your worth inside and out.

The first #araujosworldtour back in 2016 lasted for about four months. During all that time, my own mental negativity toward my body kept me from posting pictures of the most amazing places. It kept me from dressing to the occasion; instead, I hid myself in loose clothing.

Some days I actively stopped my husband from exercising because I felt bad about my own body and I didn't want him getting more fit. It was easier to convince him just to go out for drinks and dinner and continue the downward spiral the following morning, again feeling bad and repeating the process, than facing my own demons. How sad is that? How sad is it that we are so programmed to hate on ourselves if we don't look like the model on the cover picture? Hell, not even SHE looks like that—she's been Photoshopped!! Let's be honest here, we all have stretch marks!

We got back from that trip 20 pounds heavier. By that point, I had made peace with the fact that I gained a lot of weight while overseas; but what else are you supposed to do on vacation? Not eat pizza in Italy or fried rice and dumplings in China? How about stuffing your face with bread and cheese in Paris or eating all the sushi you can in Tokyo? So, while I wasn't loving the way I looked, I was at peace with the fact that it was vacation weight and that I was going to get rid of it as soon as we got back into our regular routine. Still, a lot of pictures never made it to social media out of shame. I have to say that once we arrived, I was actually pretty proud of my mom. It took her two hours after her initial look at me and a story about a great paella in Barcelona to even mention the weight! Yay, Mom!

The next six months were a struggle of their own. I went to see a nutritionist to try to get a healthy diet going. Then I went to see another one. Then I started a diet I read online. I also started an exercise routine that I hated, but "deserved" for gaining so much weight. All the while, I felt fat and unworthy of my new clothes because of my old motto of "buy clothes your ideal size so you'll get motivated to fit into them" ... It's was very sad in retrospect. During this weight-loss phase, we took one of the most wonderful trips—one of our most spontaneous yet—to Peru, to climb Machu Picchu. We didn't really climb it—we took a very nice train to the top ;). Anyway, the same story as the Great Wall of China repeated. Me feeling awful with the way I looked, Yahir frustrated that I didn't like any pictures, and a single picture out of 100s of takes made it to Facebook—and that picture only after some editing to make me look "better." Yes, by better, I mean thinner.

It wasn't until a couple of months later, lots of reading, researching, trial and error, and finally understanding that I needed to feed myself for health, not to lose weight, that my mindset started to shift. I realized that I needed to eat to have more energy, to keep diseases away, and to give my body what it needed to thrive everyday instead of trying to almost starve myself to lose weight. That is when, almost by accident (or destiny) I stumbled into a movement that would go on to change my life: the #bodypositivity, or #bopo, movement.

We live in a world where if a woman is successful and famous, or if she is poor and uneducated, the very first thing someone will talk about when referring to her is her weight. If she lost weight, or if she gained weight—for the successful counterpart—her recent lip injections are far more important to reporters than her latest product launch that is changing the world. It's the cold, hard, sad, and sexist reality. We are bombarded from the time we are kids to fit a certain stereotype, to be fit because anything else is simply wrong, to use the latest hair products, and face serums, and to do absolutely everything in our power— and beyond—to avoid gaining weight or looking old. That is the same in all classes of the social ladder. You can't escape it. I know I couldn't.

I grew up in a home where I was told every single day that I was fat. From the moment I turned 16 and my "baby fat" was simply "fat" to the moment I lost the weight at 23. It restarted again at 27 after putting on a few pounds and ended about a year ago when I finally put an end to the negative chatter. Fat in this context is 135 pounds at 5'4" instead of 120 pounds. I was told that I had a big belly and that it should always be tucked in, not to buy outfits that were too tight that would show it, and that my hair was too messy. I was made to feel that as a girl, no matter how hard I tried, or how much I aced at school, I would never be enough until I lost the extra weight.

Aside from the constant attacks to my self-esteem, and my own induced self-consciousness about my middle area, I was able to emerge with an even stronger self-esteem than most people. Almost every day, and in front of people, I would look at myself in the mirror and say, "WOW, God really overdid himself with me. I'm so pretty." I truly, really meant it. I always knew my worth. I always knew not to take crap from anyone and to value myself highly in every aspect. From dating to friendship to my following my own heart, I was one of the lucky ones.

It is not that easy for a lot of people. That shit can tear you apart. If you add a sister, mother, or group of friends that complement your own negative narrative about yourself, with comments like, "I don't want you wearing my stuff and stretching them," "It's time we start dieting for real," or, "Let's cheat today and tomorrow we'll hit the gym for twice the amount of time." Worst of all, "You're looking heavier. Here, try some of my diet pills/ new fad diet/exercise routine. It totally works!" These are all dangerous comments, especially the diet pills one. I've totally been there—both receiving and giving such awful advice.

The most important thing to understand is that it is not our fault or our loved one's fault; it's our culture. Diet culture is everywhere: magazines, TV, social media. Every time you see a post with a before and after picture or read a headline that says, "Try these fabulous five moves for bikini abs" or "Oprah lost 30 pounds. Here is how she did it!" you are being bombarded with diet culture. Making yourself feel like less unless you look like the Photoshopped magazine version of a particular movie star, with the right tan, right muscle, right hair color, and the most perfect background, you are, and always will be, "not enough."

This is where one of the wonderful movements of the times comes in: Body Positivity. They are all about making us understand that the way we look is perfectly fine and that is OK to love our bodies!

Body Positivity Movement

I first found out about the body positivity movement through Instagram in December 2016. I was just browsing the web and my social media, like every other day, looking for inspiration, looking at pictures, looking at my friends' posts, posts from some strangers who have the most wonderful pictures from somewhere around the world. Somewhere in this vast world of social media and Instagram, I stumbled upon one account that drew my attention immediately.

The picture was a girl in lingerie, but not what you would usually think. It wasn't the typical busty girl with the most amazing perfect body. She was just a normal girl, maybe around her early 20s, skinny, cute, no makeup on. What grabbed my attention was that she was purposely leaning to one side making the rolls on her stomach show along with the cellulite and being proud of it with the hashtag #embracethesquish. I was absolutely thrown back by such vulnerability on social media!! I've never seen people actually trying to make rolls with their stomach!! What you normally get is the complete opposite: the more perfect you can look the better. There was this girl doing the exact opposite of that, being proud, posting it, and hashtagging it. I started to read more about her and about what she was doing. It turns out she is an eating disorder survivor. She went through hell and back with her illness. She was now at this point in her recovery where she was actually teaching people to let go of diet culture and learn to love themselves and their bodies and to embrace it all—embrace your body, embrace your cellulite, embrace your *perfectly imperfect* body. She was the first hero I met in the body positivity movement. You can follow her: @nourishandeat.

EMBRACE YOUR BODY, EMBRACE YOUR CELLULITE, EMBRACE YOUR PERFECTLY IMPERFECT BODY.

After seeing that amazing Instagram account, I had to find more. I had to know more about this movement. I totally had to join. I didn't consider myself an eating disorder survivor, but I had to follow. I had to let someone else know. I had to adopt that mentality in my own life. That is when I made my second discovery. The hero @chooselifewarrior had posted the most amazing, jaw-dropping video I had ever seen. She was dancing in her underwear while being maybe 100 pounds overweight. The lesson she was teaching was so powerful—she was just dancing for the world to see. She was taking on haters' comments and negativity and showing what it is to be proud of your body—no matter your size. I stared in awe at this wonderful Australian girl!! I could not even look at myself in the mirror naked with my 20 pounds "overweight" and there she was almost naked dancing for the world to see!! I was beyond-words surprised and encouraged. She has now become one of the accounts I go online to see every single day. She brings so much happiness to my life through her posts, through her dances, and through her honesty. She's open and honest. Yes, she gets so many hater comments. She posts them and she tells everyone about them. She is barely in her early 20s, yet she has the courage of an older woman and she pushes me to accept my body and to love my body and to be happy in my own skin.

I may be butchering the main idea behind the movement. I truly encourage you to do your own research and learn more about the history of it because it is not new and it is not only about weight. It's also about inclusion and acceptance of marginalized bodies and their lack of representation in the media. It truly is the ultimate girl power movement! The main point I'm trying to make, however, is that our own negativity against our bodies, due to a lack of "perfection," has been imposed upon us. This also means that we have the power to change how we think and how we see ourselves and how we value our lives and our bodies according to what we think is right.

Your body, as it is today, is what's right. That's what matters. Accepting and loving your body is the single most important lesson that I can share with you in this book. When you learn to love yourself and to love and respect your body, there is no stopping you. No one can get in the way of a girl who is in charge of herself, her mind, and her body. No one will be able to take you down if you conquer those.

My limited knowledge of the body positivity movement has changed my life. It definitely changed the way I look at the world. I have started to notice that in my own social circles, whenever there are girls together, "diets" becomes one of the main topics. Loving yourself is never a part of it. It is always an "I hate my thighs," "I'm carrying around holiday weight," or any other negative comments toward the body. It is never ever anything positive—ever.

After finding out about the BOPO movement, I realized that there's so much more to life and so much more to self-acceptance than trying to be the perfect shape or trying to fit this stereotypical image of some Photoshopped girl on a magazine cover. It's really about accepting and loving your body and your mind.

I encourage you to go and follow these girls who've made my whole vision of the world shift for the better. They have saved me from spending the next 30 years worrying about my weight. I can just stare at the mirror and love what is looking back at me. Check @nourishandeat, @chooselifewarrior, and you can't miss the dances and the AMAZING HAIR and positivity of @bodyposipanda—her YouTube videos MAKE MY WORLD A BETTER PLACE!

Let's get one thing straight: accepting your body as it is today is not about not wanting to improve yourself. That implies that you are wrong somehow and are simply learning to live with it. Rather, it is about loving yourself so much, feeling so much love for your body, and feeling so grateful to have your body, that the only possible option that you have is to do better BY you. To feed yourself with what your body needs to thrive and to have energy! To move your muscles to get stronger and keep up with you conquering the world! It also means to rest and to connect with yourself. The one priority is that YOU are OK. To make yourself be the best you can because everything you'll do from now on is going to be out of love for yourself, for your body, and for your mind.

I've said it before and I'll say it again: no more judging yourself, your thoughts, your body. You are perfect! Your body is perfect the way it is. It's so crazy when people write a magazine article

LET'S GET ONE THING STRAIGHT: ACCEPTING YOUR BODY AS IT IS TODAY IS NOT ABOUT NOT WANTING TO IMPROVE YOURSELF. THAT IMPLIES THAT YOU ARE WRONG SOMEHOW AND ARE SIMPLY LEARNING TO LIVE WITH IT. RATHER, IT IS ABOUT LOVING YOURSELF SO MUCH, FEELING SO MUCH LOVE FOR YOUR BODY, AND FEELING SO GRATEFUL TO HAVE YOUR BODY, THAT THE ONLY POSSIBLE OPTION THAT YOU HAVE IS TO DO BETTER BY YOU.

saying, "You are one of these three body types." That's so not true. There are so many body types out there and they are all the perfect body type.

Have you seen those posts that say "beach body?" Go to the beach and have a body. You now have a beach body. You are perfect the minute you accept you and start letting go of all this awful culturally-induced BS that you somehow need to look different or be different or have a specific hair color or hairdo.

You are never ever going to feel like that again. From this moment forward, you will never ever again say anything negative to yourself about your body. You will never hate-talk while dressing or while walking on the street or while showering or when looking at yourself in the mirror on a Sunday morning with your mascara all the way down to your cheeks after a crazy night of partying.

You're pretty.

You're beautiful.

You're perfect.

This goes for all your friends, fellow girls, and tribe. You are never going to judge any other girl ever again. You are perfect and she is perfect as well. You are going to end the negative talk in your groups and with your tribe and with your family members. This may be the hardest part, but you can do it. We will all spread the word we will change the world!

Upon finding out about this movement and realizing that I had all these negative feelings about my own body and that a lot of them were induced in my own core family, I decided to make a lot of changes in my life. First, I was done eating to lose weight—for good. It was all about being healthier and stronger from now on. I also realized that I needed to stop the negative self-talk. To do that, I had a very hard conversation with my mom. I sat her down and set up. "Mom, no more asking how's the diet going. No more asking if I'm losing the extra weight. No more commenting on someone else's gaining or losing weight. That's done. It's like an easily-spread virus. Someone starts talking about the neighbor losing weight and then you get sucked into the conversation because you also noticed. That's just so wrong because we keep reaffirming to ourselves that it is wrong to gain a pound or two. In reality, who the hell cares? This is your

"MOM, NO MORE ASKING HOW'S THE DIET GOING. NO MORE ASKING IF I'M LOSING THE EXTRA WEIGHT. NO MORE COMMENTING ON SOMEONE ELSE'S GAINING OR LOSING WEIGHT. THAT'S DONE."

life. if you want to eat an apple pie every damn night, go for it. If you decide not to do that, do it because sugar is not good for you, not due to how any calories it has."

Treat Your Body Like A Temple

The concepts that I have mentioned about accepting your body as it is and to stop worrying about weight because it doesn't really matter may feel strange at first. They may feel wrong—or just weird. We are not used to this narrative of body positivity. We are not used to having someone tell us to be happy in our skin. Rather, when your girlfriend says, "Oh God, I'M SO FAT!" with the saddest tone filled with self-loathing, the first thing that comes to your mind as her best friend, is to say: "YOU ARE NOT! You look awesome in those jeans!" trying to reassure her that she most definitely doesn't look fat. Sadly, that is also reaffirming that being overweight or feeling bad is wrong. A more thoughtful answer would be simply saying, "SO WHAT? Why is that wrong? You are a goddess girl and it has nothing to do with your weight." Notice the difference? Notice how one is empowering and the other is negative?

We most definitely want the empowering narrative in our lives because that will lead us to an amazing self-confidence we never knew we could feel. Eventually, it will lead us to accomplish everything we want in this life. To get there, you must first start with conquering your own mind and accepting your reality.

Become aware of your self-talk. Are you constantly putting yourself down based on what you see in the mirror? Stop it. Stop it right now. Remember our no-judgment rule? This is where it is more important than ever. As the saying goes when you have nothing nice to say, don't say anything. So, yes, take a look at yourself. As soon as you catch yourself hating on your body and judging yourself, stop it. Become aware of the negative conversation in your head and stop it. If you can turn it into a positive statement that is awesome. If you can't, stay quiet.

Mark Manson in his book *The Subtle Art of Not Giving a F*ck* (FYI, I totally recommend it) talks about the feedback loop from hell. He states that sometimes positive self-talk can lead to negative emotions when the positive self-talk is not authentic. That ends in further deepening the initial negative thought to begin with. He gives the example of you feeling bad about not doing something. Then you say, "No, I don't have to feel bad about that. It was OK." Then you feel bad about feeling bad in the beginning. Then you feel worse than at the start, hence, the feedback loop from hell.

While I don't necessarily agree with everything that he says in the book, I have to say that this was a powerful realization. I have a habit of looking at myself in the mirror and saying how beautiful I look and how much I love myself every morning, yet there are days when I don't feel beautiful or I don't feel like the total goddess badass queen that other days I do feel. On those sad days, when I'm staring at myself and literally lying to myself about how beautiful I look, I feel bad deep down for not really feeling it. I push myself to do it and then feel worse about having to push myself. After reading his statements I changed my routine a little bit. Whenever I'm in front of the mirror and it's one of those days when I don't feel like I look like an angel that fell from heaven, I simply say to myself, "You are beautiful even if you don't feel it today. It's totally OK that you are not feeling it. Just know that you are and that I love you." You know what happens next? I FEEL AWESOME! Not because I instantly have the goddess feeling, but because I TRULY ACCEPTED my thoughts and my ideas and body and that makes me feel like a badass.

The simple act of letting myself feel the feelings, even if they are negative, has helped me accept myself even more. Let's face it, I'm not SUPERWOMAN. There are days when I don't feel like the queen of the world. Even on those days, I stand in front of the mirror and say the words. I go on with my day knowing that I truly love and accept myself and that my feelings are VALIDATED AND OK.

If you want to achieve your ultimate goals, become invincible, live the life you always imagined without a care of what others may think, you need to act on building your everlasting love with yourself. It starts with becoming aware of your self-talk and your emotions. Stop putting yourself down. Lift yourself up and accept. Accept the feelings. Accept the body. Feel the incredible never-ending love you feel for yourself.

Then take things one step further and be grateful for your body. You have one and it never ever stops working for you, so be thankful. Say it out loud and feel it. Appreciate the work it does for you and feel absolute gratitude for your body. This will lead you down a path of wanting to make the best decisions to make your body feel good.

Choose What's Right for Your Body

DISCLAIMER: I am not a nutritionist or health specialist. Please consult with a specialist before starting or making any dietary or exercise routine changes.

At this point, we are way beyond eating to get thinner and totally embracing the concept of eating to be nourished and healthy and feel awesome. Become aware of how your body feels after eating. Do you feel bloated? Are you in a total food coma? Do your feel empowered, full of energy, and ready to take on the challenges that may present in your day?

I suggest you consult with your nutritionist about the best path to nourish your body. Before you go, do a little research to make sure her (because it will obviously be another #girlboss like you) intentions are not to make you lose weight, but rather to give you the most nutritious diet regimen that will be right for your body and that will be right for you. What do I mean by this? I mean that there is no one single recipe for all. Simply make sure that the decisions you are making are with your body's best interest in mind, not so it looks better—because it already looks perfect—but to make sure it feels bulletproof!

I have to admit that I don't have a sugar tooth. I know I'm weird in this sense. My cravings? Chips. Sea salt potato chips with LOTS of hot sauce and lime. Remember, I'm Mexican after all. Why do I stop myself from eating them every day? It used to be about the weight, however, I've learned the hard way that the weight is not all. Every time I eat a bag of chips, I feel bad in my stomach. I feel bad right after and I feel bad the following morning. Not just mentally out of guilt—like I did in my previous bad-relationship-with-food-status—but physically. I know this has happened to me since I was a little kid. I would still eat chips like a crazy person when I wasn't home because of my mom's no-chips-on-weekdays rule. Her rule was about not gaining weight. When I removed weight from the equation, I started paying attention to how my body was feeling afterward and I DID NOT LIKE IT. I felt bloated. I could feel my hands twice their size due to water retention. My stomach felt ill. I ran to the bathroom as soon as I woke up (TMI, I know). Worst of all, I was not able to eat for a while as my stomach settled. HOW AWFUL IS THAT?! Why would I want to put my body through such a bad experience? More importantly, if I loved my body so much, how did submitting to such a hassle make any sense?

I made the choice to give up my beloved daily chips out of love for my body. This was only the beginning. I started really researching about what was healthy and not healthy for my own body. I consulted with specialists and finally decided to give up sugar all together. I also gave up carbs because they turn into sugar once in your body. I also do my best to keep my dairy intake to the minimum since it literally feeds cancer cells and causes bloating. I also gave up all processed food because it has so much shit added to it that some of it you can't even call food anymore. I don't buy anything in a can or processed when shopping for groceries. I switched to organic and grass-fed, no-hormone added options. When eating out, I do my best to find farm to table restaurants. I started feeling amazing!! With my body, with my energy, with myself! I love cooking and I found a website that had meal plans with my new specifications along with shopping lists and recipes. IT WAS PERFECT! I regained control of my kitchen, knew exactly what I was putting in my mouth, and I started giving my body what it needed!

Take the time to pay attention to your body. How does it feel after you've eaten a whole apple pie or a salad? You are not meant to be walking around feeling hungry or being in a food coma after each meal. Find your balance and find what works best for your body. I can't stress this enough: consult with your nutritionist and make a plan that will feed you with energy and everlasting happiness! Imagine freeing yourself of making dietary decisions based on how many calories a meal has, but rather knowing exactly what will make your body thrive and going for it! It's an amazing feeling!

This doesn't mean that you can't have cravings or that you should block them when they appear. Accept and embrace your inner self, remember? Accept that you will have them, because sugar is addictive, and so are salty snacks! This doesn't mean that I don't do it either. Just last night I had a small plate of chips with a glass of wine while relaxing after a hectic day. You know what? I felt good the following day because first, I hardly do it anymore. I drank a lot of water to help my body with water retention and I had only a small portion compared to my usual snacks. I'm still working on my mental reward system because it's still very much connected to food, but I'm a work in progress in this area as well. I enjoy my life completely and indulge from time to time, especially when out vacationing! I'm never going to say NO to pizza if I'm in Italy, and that's a personal rule! ;)

Move Your Booty

DISCLAIMER: I am not a nutritionist or health specialist. Please consult with a specialist before starting/continuing any exercise routine.

I used to think of exercising as a means to an end and the end was always the same: lose weight. Exercise in my head was just the most direct and most efficient way to look better. By better, I mean thinner or toned, of course. It was so effective and good that it was even better than eating right. Because after all, if I ate a bag of chips, I just needed to spend "an extra hour" in the gym to burn it off. In a sense, exercising for me felt like a punishment. I had to push myself hard at the gym for not being thin enough, or disciplined enough to eat right, and push myself even harder when it was summer and I had to be ready for bikini season because I had been indulging all winter. I had to punish my body for not being perfect by submitting it to exercise routines that I didn't like and dealing with the aches the following day, because "no pain, no gain."

Not just physically, but mentally it was a punishment too. I had to guilt myself into exercising because, again, I didn't look the way I was "supposed to," so I had to make myself go to the gym, even though I didn't like it. How could I possibly like it if I related it to actual torture and punishment for not having the perfect body? "Why am I not more into it?" I thought. "Everyone at the gym seems to be so consistent and loving it. What's wrong with me? I look bad. On top of that, I don't want to improve. I must be the weird one here!" I would give myself constant shit over not just being fat, but being lazy as well, and then deciding, "F it. I'm already fat; I might as well go and get some chips. It's not like anything is going to change after all." The following day the guilt trip would start all over again, some days ending in exercising, others in partying, some others in eating way too many tacos.

For a small period of time back in 2011, all that changed. I signed up for a 10K race. It wasn't a lot, but given the fact that I'd never run before, it felt like a big deal to me. I wasn't doing it because I wanted to lose weight. I was actually at my "goal weight" that year. Rather, I signed up because I wanted to challenge myself and felt like running could be fun. I was in a very good relationship with my body at that time and my only ulterior motive was to try something new.

That month of training prior to the race, I woke up at 7 am (if you know me, you'd know I don't do 7 am ...Hell! I hardly do 9 am! Ha ha!), met the training group I signed up with, and went for a run. Some days I did strength exercising. Other days, simply running. It was the most liberating experience I'd had while exercising ever. Some days I wouldn't even turn the music on, just sort of run alone with my thoughts. It felt incredible like I was running in my own little cloud while having an amazing conversation with myself *and* moving my body and feeling awesome afterwards. The day of the race I was ready. I'd been preparing. My coach said I was going to do just fine. I started to run with all my willpower as soon as the bell rang. That day was an incredible personal accomplishment and my body felt awesome after the fact. I felt invincible!

I signed up for that same race two years in a row. Both times it felt really great when I reached the finish line! That was the first time in my entire life when I wasn't exercising as a punishment or with any hidden agenda. I was simply enjoying the adrenaline rush, the introspection, and feeling incredible after being done. It would, however, take a few more years of going back to the old "exercise because you gained weight" routine before I could have that feeling again.

At the end of 2016, when I discovered the BOPO movement and made the conscious decision to stop making decisions based on weight repercussions, I had to re-examine my personal exercise routine once more just like I'd done with my eating habits. At the time, I was doing an app-based girls-only routine that promised you could have the best body in your life in 28 minutes a day. Twenty-eight please-kill-me-now-this-is-too-hard-and-I-hate-you minutes a day. I have to admit that the routine was pretty straight forward, "easy" to do at home, and, while demanding, it was effective on its promise to deliver you a great body if you followed through with the program and did your routine every day, including the rest days' stretches. The problem? I hated it. I hated it so much I would sabotage my own program every time I could and would talk myself into not waking up early enough to do it every other day. Why? You guessed it—because I was doing it once more out of hate for my body and to lose weight and have the "stereotypical perfect" body. I wasn't looking at this awesome app as a great way to blow off some steam, or for the endorphin release, but rather as yet another way to punish my body, my mind, and my overall self for not being perfect enough.

For the first 28 years of my life, I sabotaged myself out of exercising regardless of the amazing health benefits the right routine could give. Even though I felt great after a good exercise routine and my days felt awesome when I woke up early and exercised. For 28 years, however, I had looked at exercise the same way—as punishment for my lack of a perfect body and as an even more painful torture for my lack of discipline while eating.

My own mind, aided with society's expectations, had turned something so awesome as exercising into the single most dreaded minutes of my day causing me to avoid them like the plague. As soon as I linked going out for a run with losing weight, even running lost its amazing self-reflection and reality-escape features I had when running my first race.

FOR 28 YEARS, HOWEVER, I HAD LOOKED AT EXERCISE THE SAME WAY— AS PUNISHMENT FOR MY LACK OF A PERFECT BODY AND AS AN EVEN MORE PAINFUL TORTURE FOR MY LACK OF DISCIPLINE WHILE EATING.

In the awakening of my new mentality, where weight has no room in the decision-making process of any aspect of my life, I realized my body needed movement to thrive. Just like I started to notice how my body felt after each meal, I also started to notice how my body felt at the end of each day. Back pains from sitting down all day, muscle loss from having starved myself for that last wedding I attended, lack of energy half-way through my day, and a sense of disconnection with my body. Not even once in my life, had I done a single exercise routine with my body's health as the focal point. That had to change immediately. This is when I discovered yoga.

To me, yoga is a way of communicating with my body, with my breath, and with myself. It's way more than just stretching or holding a pose. It's a full-on trip inside myself where I take time-out from life and give my body my full attention thus becoming aware of its needs, its lacks, and its accomplishments.

After completing my first-ever yoga routine through an app, I felt at home. I could feel myself so completely in sync with my body that I started to notice everything about it. I felt my back pain disappear. I could feel muscles I didn't even know existed were now stretched and happy. I could feel my own breath in sync with my movements.

Yoga was the routine I never knew I always needed.

I felt like I had finally found my passion. After 30 minutes, I finally understood why all those people in my old gym would happily and willingly go every day, or those runners continue to do it every day for years, and even why everyone I knew seemed really to "enjoy" going to the gym when I used to hate it.

There was nothing wrong with exercising or with my previous routines. The problem had always been in my head. After almost 30 years of feeling like the only person who didn't like working out in the world because everyone else seemed to enjoy it so damn much, I finally got it. For the first time ever, I had a workout routine that I looked forward to, that I enjoyed, and that I could see the results of day after day. Results were happiness, a relaxed yet full-of-energy body, and a complete self-awareness of what my body needed.

It has been over a year and a half since that first morning routine and still I look forward every day to my yoga time. Sometimes it's in the morning, sometimes in the evening, sometimes in the middle of the day when my thoughts are all over the place and I need to feel grounded, or simply before going to bed when I need to relax. I found my place in the workout universe and I'm never letting go.

Moving your body for the purpose of making it feel great, release endorphins, feel incredible energy and utter love for your body is one of the most self-loving actions you can take. It goes hand in hand with eating what's right for you and it's a key aspect of treating your body like a temple.

Remember, you only get one body; love it and listen to it when is asking you for a break or a stretch. Find the perfect routine for you. It could be yoga like it was for me, but it could also be salsa, Crossfit, boxing, running, heavy lifting, Zumba, or whatever else makes you happy and truly inspires you to do it every day way beyond the aesthetic results. The inner results will show on the outside by how much self-confidence you exude due to so many endorphins running around in your system and how your muscles never ache from inactivity, but are ready to conquer the world with you.

Never Dress Out of Shame

Have you ever had one of those mornings where you have "nothing to wear?" The closet is full of clothes, however, that day the stars most definitely didn't align and nothing fits right. You blame your stupid clothes. You go on and on about how badly you need to go shopping. Then you blame yourself for not having the time. Then you blame yourself for not being able to afford it. Then you blame yourself for looking bad in everything and just know that if you only lost a pound or two everything would be different.

"Victoria Beckham never goes through this in the morning" you think...while still hating the image in the mirror. In the end, you put on an outfit that worked last week. Today, it just simply makes you look horrible, but you ran out of time, curse one more time at the mirror, and head out the door hoping you don't run into anyone your know, especially your ex and his new beautiful girlfriend. You spend the rest of the day hiding at work because your feel completely uncomfortable and you don't want anyone seeing how big your arms look in that shirt. Let me start by saying, it happens to all of us, and yes, Victoria goes through this, too.

When all this is happening and you're in the middle of your existential crisis over ripped jeans or black leggings, have you ever stopped for a second and thought to yourself, "Who am I dressing for today?" Why on that particular day your favorite shirt just didn't seem to work, or was it the shoes? I've found that these mornings are usually always aligned with one of the days I'm not feeling like the most beautiful goddess and I'm trying to be someone I'm not.

What do I mean by that? I mean that whenever I'm getting ready for the day, be it to go meet a client, go grocery shopping, go on date night, or even just to run errands, the amount of time I will spend choosing what to wear, and then changing it one gazillion times before settling in on the very first outfit I tried on is directly related to whom I am trying to impress.

Sometimes it's the hubby. Sometimes it's a coworker. Sometimes it's the cute guy at the store. Other times it's someone I'm about to meet—a friend's new girlfriend or wife, or just the girlfriends. Whenever I'm dressing for someone other than myself, and that particular day I'm not feeling like a goddess, I end up kicking myself upon returning home. Why? Because a lack of authenticity along with a lack of self-confidence is usually a recipe for disaster.

Recently, I was invited to a Christmas party with some of my husband's work acquaintances. I had no idea who these people were, what age group they were in or how boringly-grown-up they would be, so I struggled a lot with what to wear for the event.

I did my due diligence and went shopping ahead of time to avoid the "I-hate-my-closet" situation right before the event. I actually got lucky and found the most perfect dress to wear in the season's trending color that made me look pretty hot. It was sexy yet classy.

Perfect.

I also found the most funny and cool ornament-shaped earrings to go with it! I thought they were so perfect for the occasion and they were funny and complemented my dress perfectly. Shopping was a wrap.

The day of the event arrived and I started having second thoughts about my Christmas-themed earrings. "What if these people were more serious than that? I mean they could've thrown an ugly sweater party if they were fun, however, they decided to rent a bar. They must be more grown-up than I'm thinking....

What if my dress is too short?

Does it look too "Pretty Woman" with my above-the-knee heels?

Maybe I should just put on some tights and heels instead... but who wears tights anymore? They've been out of style for at least two years...What would my mom think? Maybe I should opt for classy versus hot..."

I was in the middle of my mental argument with myself when my hubby walks in and says "WOW! You look great!" PHEW! "He likes it!" I thought, "Why do I even care what anybody else thinks?" So, I kept my original sexy/classy outfit, but I still couldn't force myself to wear the ornament earrings. I loved them. I loved how they looked and I loved how they complemented the dress perfectly, but I was still very much concerned with giving a good first impression and decided to not wear them. I put on a different pair of earrings, more boring ones, and headed out.

After a couple of hours at the event, I was having a great time. I had received a few compliments on my outfit, high-fived my inner self for sticking with what I wanted, and felt like I could just be myself around these people, however, there was a major rock in my shoe. Walking around the party, was a guy that had dyed his beard green, and had mini-ornaments hanging from it. I started to kick myself mentally. He had decided to own it. He decided to own what he wanted to do, for whatever reason he wanted to do it. Maybe it was just attention. In any case, he decided to go for it, while my beautiful earrings that were a perfect match to my dress were sitting in my dresser and I was wearing this boring set... "This is never happening to me again," I thought. "Why didn't I just go with my instinct and wear what I truly wanted?"

This happens every time we dress for someone else instead of dressing for ourselves. In the end, who really cares what we wear? I don't think anyone is really paying that much attention. If they are, we might never find out, so why bother? Why not instead use it to lift ourselves up instead of using it to portray some image that doesn't really align with our truth? Keep in mind that you are a multifaceted person and you are allowed to have multiple personalities aligning with who you truly are.

One day you may feel like a rock star.

Other days, you may feel like a librarian.

Other days you might just feel like a surfer girl-next-door type of girl.

All of them are correct for your day. Dress up for the occasion. The occasion is you being you, being present in your life, and being true to yourself. That calls for a toast!

Remember the story of when I was on the Great Wall of China and no picture was good enough? That morning I was feeling fat. I was feeling anything but pretty, and I was severely hungover from clubbing the night before (nightlife in China can get pretty wild). I was feeling guilty for succumbing to the munchies in the middle of the night making my fat-phobia increase. I woke up feeling like crap. The tour was picking us up really early to take us to the wall and I had no intention of paying attention to myself that day.

I remember opening up the closet, looking at what was left in the "clean clothes" section and grabbing the largest, loosest fitting top I could find. I contrasted that with a pair of leggings that wouldn't be too tight on my middle section, put on my sunglasses, a hat for the sun, and walked out the door thinking, "I look awful, but at least no one knows me here." You know how that turned out.

That morning I had dressed to hide myself. I was projecting how bad I felt about my body on the inside by not making any effort to look good on the outside. On the contrary, I was actively trying to hide myself relying on the fact that I was not meeting anyone so, why bother?

This is just as bad a problem as dressing up for someone else. When we are dressing for someone else, or worse, hiding ourselves from ourselves because we can't stand to look in the mirror on days like this, the only result we obtain is putting ourselves down. We feel way worse than at the beginning. We freeze ourselves from taking any action that will lead us to achieving our goals or to owning our future because we can't own ourselves. Instead, we are too busy hiding and judging ourselves. We are either caught up on a fake portrayal of ourselves that doesn't let our true selves and our true aspirations shine—since the portrayal doesn't really align with the image—or we let our insecurities take the best of us and end up wearing whatever will make us invisible to everyone around us resulting in us feeling too invisible to act and stand up for ourselves.

If you catch yourself dressing to hide yourself, or giving yourself shit on how bad you look, stop it. Stop these horrible practices that become worse with every passing day. Every morning when you are getting ready and start having second thoughts, or feeling ugly/fat/deformed or whatever insecurity is crawling up, ask yourself,

- Who am I dressing up for?
- What am I dressing up for?
- Am I dressing up to lift myself up or to give myself confidence?
- To show off how amazingly good I feel about myself?
- To show off my incredible personality?
- Am I hiding myself?

- Maybe I'm dressing up to impress someone else.
- Since I don't read minds, is it causing me to second guess everything I choose?

Acceptance is a word that I've repeated a million times in this book so far, but its power is beyond words. Accept your body, your mind, your worth. Even accept your insecurities—we all have them. Don't let them control how you show up in the world. Don't let your own inner monsters cripple you from feeling like the ultimate badass and showing it by how you dress, how you walk, and how you talk and act.

Dress however YOU want to. Dress for yourself. Be as authentic on your outer self as you are on your inner self. Never judge yourself or others. When deciding what to wear, always take a moment and understand how you feel that day: insecure or ultra-confident? Maybe in between? Maybe lazy. The way you feel will affect what you pick.

I suggest dressing up in confidence, both inside and out, even if you may not be feeling it. Dress to lift yourself up. Overdress if you are feeling under, so you'll look in the mirror and say, "DAMN! I'm hot!" Wear your most amazing stilettos that make you feel sexy on days when you need it. Wear your big combat boots if you feel like those give you the courage to take on the world. Maybe wear your Hello, Kitty purse that makes you feel like your most authentic self ever.

Never, ever, let your demons win!

It's OK to feel awful some days. It's OK and normal to feel imperfect. Let those feeling sink in. Embrace them and then move on. It is NOT OK to let them linger and control your life. Never let them rule your world.

I'm still a work in progress in this area. It's a daily battle; however, every time I'm about to succumb to my insecurities, I remember that day in China where they almost stopped me from seeing an amazing heritage of civilization and I reaffirm to myself that I'll never go through that ever again. I know better now. I know that my body is my temple and that there is no room for self-hate in my mental chatter. I love myself too much for that. I'm perfect in my imperfect self just as I am. I'm beautiful. I'm invincible. I have no idea how much I weigh. Even if I did, that number no longer means anything at all in my path.

I've come a long way since I was 16 and hating on my body for not being the perfect shape, or on my hair for not being straight "like everyone else's." (I made peace with my hair at 18 and it is now BY FAR what I love most about myself.) I've come a long way since hating on my own mind for allowing all these

IT'S OK TO FEEL AWFUL SOME DAYS. IT'S OK AND NORMAL TO FEEL IMPERFECT. LET THOSE FEELINGS SINK IN. EMBRACE THEM AND THEN MOVE ON. IT IS NOT OK TO LET THEM LINGER AND CONTROL YOUR LIFE. NEVER LET THEM RULE YOUR WORLD.

negative feelings to surface. I've been burned and cried and grown and realized that the problem lies outside of us with diet culture monopolizing how we are supposed to look. Our own families and societal expectations enforce it for us as women on a daily basis.

I've also learned that the *real* change has to come from within. We have the power to remove these archaic ideas from our heads, from our conversations, and from our lives. We can truly change the world if we all stop succumbing to the sexist ideas and Photoshopped images. It is within us. It is within you that you'll find your biggest supporter, your biggest ally, or your worst enemy. You decide every single day through conscious or unconscious decisions which one you are going to listen to today. If you can conquer your mind and fall in love with yourself, you can conquer and change your world. If you have only one take-away from this book, let it be that.

CHINA

CHINA

CHAPTER 5

Letting Go Of Other People's Expectations

" "I had two cars repossessed and I was writing bad checks, but I gave myself a timeline," she recalled. "I thought, 'OK, if I don't make it by 25, I'm just going to get married and pop out some babies and do some crafts.'" – Katy Perry

I adore Katy Perry. I find her authentic and unapologetic. She grew up in a Christian household out of which she completely rebelled to become a pop star diva using sexually themed songs and flashy outfits. Talk about making a 180! She most definitely didn't do what was expected of her. She decided to bet on herself, discovered who she truly was, and showed up in full authenticity to her life. She achieved one of her biggest dreams in spite of the many, many, many roadblocks and doubters. She let go of what others thought, including her own family and pastor parents, and went on to make out of life whatever she wanted. She is still doing it today.

What would have happened if she'd given up or if she'd listened to everyone who told her that it was an impossible dream? What about succumbing to what her parents originally wanted for her life to be a good Christian? Maybe they wanted her to follow through with the promise to get married, pop out some kids, and be a good wife. Why can't she be both? Why does she need to fit into some box? Why do I keep asking questions about her life? She is doing whatever she wants. Who cares what I think?

That is the point.

In the end, the real difference between those who seem to be living the life of their dreams and those who seem stuck is the importance they give to what other people think. I once read a post that said, "What will people say? This sentence has killed more dreams than anything else in the world."

We spend so much energy trying to achieve our dreams, but we waste even more worrying about what other people might think. The math is not working in our favor. The reality is, you'll never be able to please everyone around you, but is not your fault for trying.

We are programmed to be people pleasers. We are told from the time we are young to be good girls, to behave and to do as we are told, not to call too much attention to ourselves, to follow the rules, and to do our best to fit into our role in society. Even though it's not your fault that you were raised like most of us to be good girls, IT IS your responsibility to drop that BS and create a new narrative for yourself.

Don't be a good girl. Be an authentic girl. Don't do what other people tell you to do. Do what feels right for you. Don't behave according to the rules. Behave according to your truth and your values. Go ahead, call attention to yourself, make sure everyone listens when you say, "This is who I am and I'm not changing for

DON'T BE A GOOD GIRL. BE AN AUTHENTIC GIRL. DON'T DO WHAT OTHER PEOPLE TELL YOU TO DO. DO WHAT FEELS RIGHT FOR YOU. DON'T BEHAVE ACCORDING TO THE RULES. BEHAVE ACCORDING TO YOUR TRUTH AND YOUR VALUES.

anyone." Create your own role in society curated to your unique self. Stop trying to fit in and opt for standing out by being just like Katy Perry: authentic and unapologetic.

Live the Life of YOUR Dreams

Cancun is a city of dreamy beaches, all-inclusive resorts, and incredible nightclubs with music that never stops. It's also the location of my wedding. I never really gave much thought to wedding planning while growing up, as I know other girls do. I didn't fantasize about the big day, an amazing white dress, flowers and center pieces, or a live band versus DJ.

"When am I going to take my first sabbatical and travel through Europe?" was the theme of most of my daydreams.

Even without the planning, the day most girls dream of arrived. Yahir got down on one knee, took out the most beautiful engagement ring I'd ever seen, and popped the question. I started crying hysterically. Maybe I did dream of this moment after all. Finally, after a couple of heart-stopping minutes, I said, "Yes!"

That first moment, I was beyond words excited, happy, crying, out of myself in bliss, and utterly in love. The next few days, we made the announcement. Then I had to start planning a wedding I'd never thought of.

The only thing I did know was that I wanted it to be at the beach.

For a brief period of time, everything seemed to take shape and it looked like things were falling in place when my parents told us that they wanted to help out with the wedding and that they'd pay for the venue.

This turned out to be a double-edged sword, however.

Their incredible generosity also meant that they had a say on the wedding decisions. While I was incredibly grateful for their help and their desires to make my dreams a reality, I also didn't want anyone to have an opinion on my wedding. Not even Yahir (ha ha), though I HAD to listen to *his* ideas at least.

Even though my parents' gift was an amazing one, I eventually decided to turn it down and do things my way. The wedding they wanted to help us pay for was a big wedding, with all of our family and friends in a beautiful beach retreat near my hometown. It looked like it could've been a dream wedding, however, I wanted to get married at the beach.

That was a problem for our priest since Catholic weddings can't take place outside of church. I also didn't really care for a large wedding. I just wanted my close friends and family to be with us while we got married on the beach and then we'd just party. Not too much planning.

That is when I found the one: the church, I mean. In a certain beachfront hotel in the Cancun hotel-zone lies an almost hidden chapel that sits right above the white sand overlooking the beautiful Caribbean water and it's made entirely of glass. It was the closest thing to getting married right on the sand as a Catholic that I was going to find. It was incredibly beautiful in its perfect location with the waves as a background. The dream came true, I thought. The problem? Everyone and everything.

You see, having a destination wedding is a very popular idea; lots of couples do it every day. This particular venue, however, wasn't adequate for larger parties. Neither the place nor our budget wanted the original 200 guests to attend. What did I want and what could I afford? Our closest friends and family. This presented an issue with my family.

"How are you not going to invite your extended family?"

"What am I supposed to say to my cousins?"

"Not everyone is going to be able to afford it."

"You are being selfish and only thinking of yourself."

Yes, Mom, that is exactly what I was thinking—about myself, about my wedding day, and about what I wanted for my special day.

It took A LOT of willpower not to cave to those comments and to the following months of guilt trips about how selective the list of guests was.

In the end, we had the most amazing dream wedding I could have possible imagined. Roughly 40 guests managed to follow us on our crazy Cancun wedding idea. My parents had an incredible vacation and helped out with the video. We all had an amazing time and I still remember that weekend as the best weekend in my life.

We had the right group of people for the event. We partied, drank, toasted, took a mini road trip to Playa del Carmen after the reception. It was an incredible vibe with the right crew. We were all together for four days and we had the time of our lives!!

Everyone who agreed to make the trip and spend money attending our wedding TRULY wanted to be there because they were our real tribe! They were not just guests making an appearance to be polite. We didn't invite them only to be polite, but because we truly wanted them to be there. That is exactly what I wanted and I got it—against a lot of doubters.

Could I have made my life easier during those planning months by just caving? Yes. Would my wedding had been awesome? Most likely, yes. Would I have done it only to make my mom happy? YES. Do I regret my decision? NOT IN THE SLIGHTEST.

You get one life and you have to make it count for YOU.

Letting go of what other people expect of you in order to prioritize your own dreams and wishes may be seen as selfish, but the best thing you can do for others is to live your life to your full potential. If you make your life everything you've ever wished it to be, you are automatically giving permission to those around you to do with their lives whatever they've always wanted as well. You are becoming an example of a life well lived, and a person truly fulfilled. You'll be in a far better position to help others when you know you are doing what you want with your life.

People Pleasing

As we covered in the past chapters, the key to achieving the life you've always imagined is to get clarity in what that life looks like, accepting that as your reality, and moving forward each day until you obtain it. In action though, that is far easier said than done.

Why? Because we have imprinted in our minds, even the most self-confident of us, to care at some level about making those around us happy, especially those close to us. This, however, is as counterproductive as it gets. The more you achieve your own

LETTING GO OF WHAT OTHER PEOPLE EXPECT OF YOU IN ORDER TO PRIORITIZE YOUR OWN DREAMS AND WISHES MAY BE SEEN AS SELFISH, BUT THE BEST THING YOU CAN DO FOR OTHERS IS TO LIVE YOUR LIFE TO YOUR FULL POTENTIAL. IF YOU MAKE YOUR LIFE EVERYTHING YOU'VE EVER WISHED IT TO BE, YOU ARE AUTOMATICALLY GIVING PERMISSION TO THOSE AROUND YOU TO DO WITH THEIR LIVES WHATEVER THEY'VE ALWAYS WANTED AS WELL.

potential, the more you fulfill your dreams, the more you can be who you are meant to be and want to be, the more you'll make those around you proud of you, not the opposite.

This also may feel counterintuitive, since all your mom really wants for you is to get married to a good man and have kids, right? You might as well just do it. The reality is not that simple. When you choose yourself, embrace your own dreams, and become your true self, in spite of her (or anyone else's) ideas and expectations, she will be proud.

When you choose to travel the world instead of popping out kids, she will be the first one to share that with the entire world and to talk about it to whomever will listen. She'll talk to her friends about how your trip to the Taj Mahal was magical or to strangers about how you went to Dubai to stand at the top of the tallest building in the world.

Will she still have more expectations for you? Always. Do you need to accomplish them to make her happy? Not really; you've already proven that. Even if she never says it to your face, I promise you she will be proud.

People pleasing is a rigged game, especially given the fact that you can't read minds. The only one that will keep losing is you. You'll be sacrificing what you truly want in order to do what you think other people may want from you. You will never

WHEN YOU GIVE 100% TO YOU, YOU'LL ACHIEVE A LEVEL OF HAPPINESS AND FULFILLMENT YOU NEVER THOUGHT POSSIBLE, YET YOU ALWAYS CRAVED. YOU'LL WAKE UP EACH DAY EAGER AND EXCITED TO LIVE YOUR LIFE BECAUSE IT'S THE LIFE YOU ALWAYS IMAGINED.

live up to others' expectations. Even if you do, you won't be happy since you won't be living up to your own. You have a certain amount of time in this world. Make sure not to waste it going around worrying about what other people think—you can't control that.

Instead, worry about the things that are in your power: your job, your income, your relationships, your daily actions, your future, your happiness. Spend all your energy working on those things, on improving them, on changing them as necessary, on growing, and on helping others. Never waste it on making sure you are living up to someone else's expectations. You're either following your dreams or helping others follow theirs.

Respect yourself to the point where you would never let someone else's opinion of you become your reality. You know exactly who you are, what you want, how much you're worth, and you know better than to worry about what other people may think.

When you give 100% to you, you'll achieve a level of happiness and fulfillment you never thought possible, yet you always craved. You'll wake up each day eager and excited to live your life because it's the life you always imagined.

You are working on your passions. You've surrounded yourself with those who truly care for you and you've let go of the petty things and energy-robbers. You've freed yourself to worry about only the things that truly matter—like achieving your lifelong dreams, loving yourself, and maybe also buying that cute dress your never thought you'd pull off yet makes you look like a total goddess.

Make those your biggest worries and you'll never look back.

Setting Boundaries

As much as I want to say to you that the road to living a well-fulfilled life, loving yourself, and achieving all of your dreams will be met by never-ending support from lovers, family, and friends who will cheer you on and be there to celebrate your success and failures, the reality is that won't be the case. At least not on its own.

You may have a group of friends who are 100% behind you and push you to be better. You may have a boyfriend, husband, or lover that loves nothing but to see you happy and will give you his shoulder to cry on every time you get a rejection and a family who has always believed in you and is always ready to do anything for you in a matter of seconds when you need them. You, my friend, are incredibly lucky and should nourish those relationships because they are not easy to come by. Be forever grateful and make sure you are always there for them as well.

For many, that is not your life. Maybe your friends are awesome to party with, but when it's time to share your dreams in life, they make fun of you or completely disregard your ideas as dumb or silly and they encourage you to follow the "normal" path. Maybe they would rather talk about last night's party than your true aspirations and will judge you all the way.

Maybe the guy you are hanging out with all the time is only there for you when HE needs it, not necessarily just for sex, but only for him to talk about his ideas and dreams, and when it's your turn he always has a call to take, somewhere else to be, or is too tired to listen.

Maybe it's your family members. Maybe your sister will listen to your ideas and dreams, however, she may or may not understand them. Her answer is always the same, "Grow up already. You should just go back to doing what you know. Just get a job and start saving for a car/house/wedding like everyone else."

If one of these is true for you, then it's time to do a deep soul-search and go back to "Why am I hanging out with these people?" Maybe it started when you were younger. Maybe they've been your friends since high school. Maybe the guy is cute and sometimes does seem to care; maybe the sex is just too good.

You are, however, a different person now from when you were back in college and those "friends" are not compatible with you anymore. Maybe you are starting to realize that if you are sharing your bed with a guy, he should respect you enough to listen to what you have to say and actually care about you. Your sister may have her heart in the right place, but if she is not truly supportive of what you are trying to accomplish, maybe she is not the person to open your heart to.

It's time to set boundaries with those who won't cheer you on your way to self-discovery and success. At this point in your life, you are old enough to know who is adding to your life and who is just simply robbing you of your time and energy—pushing you down to make themselves feel better. Those people have no room in your life anymore, even if it's hard to accept.

THOSE PEOPLE HAVE NO ROOM IN YOUR LIFE ANYMORE, EVEN IF IT'S HARD TO ACCEPT.

With all honesty and a hand to your heart, ask yourself,

- Who is really there for you?
- Who is honest?
- Who has no issues giving you tough love if it means it will make you grow?
- Who celebrates your victories?
- Who drinks with you to your failures?
- Who truly wants to see you succeed in whatever you decide to do?

Don't make the mistake of believing they are your friends. They might not be anymore, if they ever were. Cut ties with the negative people in your life. Make a point of avoiding those who will only bring you down. Start with one month taking the challenge at the end of this book. Take a four-weeks detox of those people and see how you feel.

How much do you truly miss them? How much happier can you be without them?

Spend that extra time and energy showering yourself with love and surrounding yourself with your real friends and supportive family members. Spend the time growing and embracing who you truly are. Find support in those who truly care for you, even if it means that you have only one person left in your inner circle.

In the case where the people you need to take a break from are your family members, it may not be as easy to simply "cut them from your life," however, you can choose to spend the least amount of time possible with them—maybe just at the previously-scheduled family dinner. Even then, see if you can avoid it altogether. Dad will understand if it's just one time.

Even if you are forced to face them during this trial period, that doesn't necessarily mean that you need to spill the beans and tell them everything you've been up to. Be polite, be friendly, but be distant. You don't need to be their best friend just because you're family, especially if they are not interested in your well-being.

There will always be an aunt, cousin, long lost friend-of-the-family that never hesitates to ask you something personal, stereotypical, and somewhat judgmental. You've worked too hard to remove those last-century ideas from your mind to give them permission to put them back in your head.

- "When are you guys plan on having your first kid? You've been married four years now; it's time!"

- "Does your husband HELP you around the house? He is such a keeper."
- "You're looking really good. What kind of diet are you on now? It works!"
- "You should get a friend for your cousin. She needs to get married asap."

There are two ways I deal with this type of behavior. The first, and least confrontational, is to smile and nod. Better used when the person is your grandmother or an elder whom you want not to disrespect, regardless of the question being offensive.

I learned the smile and nod routine to practice during family reunions through the better part of a decade. When confronted with this type of question, you simply smile, nod, and say something like, "Right? Oh, let me go get another drink/more food/go to the bathroom." Then you quickly walk away and do not come back to this person.

Polite and effective. The person will probably continue discussing it behind your back, so feel free to make conversation with someone less intrusive.

The other method? Dropping a #truthbomb.

"Does your husband HELP around the house?" Smile and then drop the bomb: "He doesn't HELP me; it's both our responsibility to have a clean house, it's not 1955 anymore..." *cue for shocked faces* "Oh, let me go get another drink/more food/go to the bathroom," and again, walk away.

Kids? "Never."

Diet? "Not obsessing over weight anymore."

Cousin? "She is free to do whatever she wants with her life. Leave her alone."

This type of answer usually stops them cold. They look at you with a sort of shock and surprise and then they never ask you again.

Win-win.

I use a combination of both, or one or the other. It really depends on my mood or who is asking the question.

Remember that you don't need to be pushed into a conversation about how you are not making the right choices in your life or how someone else is doing better than you. Always remember that the first step to owning your future and creating the life you truly want is to respect and love yourself even if it means defending yourself from anyone who is ready to put you down, regardless of who it is—a stranger, your grandmother, or your not-so-friendly friends.

Online Tribe

However lonely this may feel, remember that you don't need to walk this path alone. If after taking a long look at your current circle you realize there are only a few true friendships, or maybe none, remember that we live in the age of technology.

Your tribe, and your escape from the harshness of real life, can be on the other side of the screen. Stop following dumb accounts that only make you feel bad about yourself, that support diet culture and stereotypes, or bring women down in general. Start following people who empower you to be better and to follow your dreams. Analyze how you are spending your online time.

STOP FOLLOWING DUMB ACCOUNTS THAT ONLY MAKE YOU FEEL BAD ABOUT YOURSELF, THAT SUPPORT DIET CULTURE AND STEREOTYPES, OR BRING WOMEN DOWN IN GENERAL. START FOLLOWING PEOPLE WHO EMPOWER YOU TO BE BETTER AND TO FOLLOW YOUR DREAMS.

Who are you interacting with the most? If it's with the same negative crowd as you do in real life, change that. It has the same effect on social media as it does in person. Make sure you have an online escape that will uplift you as soon as you open your phone instead of one that will make you doubt everything you are doing. Let's face it, Instagram takes up 90% of your day.

I've started a community of girls just like you and me where no judgment is allowed and where we get together to bring each other up, to discuss how to improve ourselves, how to deal with roadblocks, with negative people, and particularly to give each other the courage and accountability we all need to achieve the life of our dreams, on our own terms, on our own times, and whatever that means to any of us. We are all on the same boat, so no one has to go through this process alone. We are your tribe to rely on when you want to share your successes with people who will understand or when you need a word of encouragement after your mom asked for the millionth time when are you going to settle down or just to share a laugh because you had one too many glasses of wine. Go to momisnotalwaysright. com/resources and ask to join our community of like-minded girls ready to become the cheerleading squad on your path to self-discovery and self-love. We are all here for you.

There is one rule, though. As part of your contract upon signing up, you agree that you won't judge anyone in the group. You won't put down anyone. Dieting comments are not allowed. On the contrary, you are to comment positive and uplifting thoughts on your sisters' questions and ramblings. More importantly, as you will receive never-ending support from all of us, you are obligated to give your support by commenting on a post when you have the right answer, or reassuring the doubter girl who just had a bad day, and making sure to check in at least twice a week to make sure you are sharing your path with us, because we truly want to know! If you can handle this, go ahead to *momisnotalwaysright.com/resources*. Leave a post introducing yourself to us. Let us in on your challenges and we will be sure to reply! I can't wait to hear from you!

CANCUN

CANCUN

REBEL LIFESTYLE DESIGN STEP 2

RADICAL CLARITY

CHAPTER 6

Rebel Lifestyle Design Advanced

When I made the decision to write this book, a lot of things were happening in my life. We had just returned from our first #araujosworldtour and I was back at work like nothing had happened.

I encountered tons of questions and shock from almost everybody about how we made such a magical trip possible, about the money required, actually taking the time to do it, and even some friends asked me about how to convince their husbands to jump on board with their own dreams...

Now back in real life and in the same old routine, I couldn't help but feel like something was missing. I'd put my hand in the cookie jar and I wasn't ready to let that go.

I had experienced a life of true freedom and true adventure. Most importantly, I had listened to my gut and followed my instincts fully to do all the stuff I had always dreamed of. My soul and heart were as happy as you can imagine.

I had embraced my dreams, accepted them, and stopped at nothing until I finally was able to make them a reality for those four months.

I wanted more.

I didn't just want it to be a one-time experience, but my way of life. Yahir agreed.

So, I did what I do best. I put my heart and soul into researching how to make that happen. I read books, blogs, followed influencers, you name it. After many hours and weeks spent, I realized that writing for profit could be the solution. It could possibly bring in passive income so I wouldn't have to work, and we could just spend our time traveling. Amazing idealistic dream, right? I read about it in *The 4-Hour Work Week* by Tim Ferriss. "Hell, if he could do it, so can I!" I thought.

That journey of writing, however, took many faces and ups and downs. At first, I thought I could write a book about interior design; I mean, that is what I did for a living. Then I realized I wasn't as passionate about that as I was about traveling. Then I thought I could do a traveling blog where I could discuss points and miles. I signed up for WordPress, bought a domain, and wrote two or three posts that never went live. It was just so new to me.

As much as I loved traveling, other things started occupying my mind. I got new clients, my job was going great, and we were able to take mini trips to give us a "quick-fix" to our traveling addiction.

AGAIN WITH THE EXPECTATIONS. AGAIN WITH TRYING TO PUT US IN A BOX.

I realized that if this ever would become a reality, I needed more time to focus fully on my dreams and my goals and to achieve the life I wanted and had seen possible. I talked to my manager in the 9 – 5. Being the awesome person that he is, he agreed to me coming in only part-time. That freed up my time! ...I thought.

After attending a live event, doing further reading, and researching on writing opportunities, I decided I wanted to write a book, not a blog. I fell in love with the idea of a book! I loved writing and a book sounded like the most awesome way to share all my thoughts on a subject! A book about traveling, maybe about marriage, maybe about living outside of the status quo. I was onto something real for the first time! I even made it as far as writing an outline and writing two of the chapters.

I let my own insecurities and life get in the way. After a month or so of writing, I let other projects become a priority. My morning routine no longer included writing, but designing. The days I had off at my job, which were meant for writing, were now being spent on design projects and client meetings.

Almost eight months went by like this. I felt exhausted. I felt burnt out. I felt like I was not heading toward my ideal life. I was craving an escape. I needed to get a way. I wanted to go to the airport and take a flight to anywhere.

We had been taking monthly weekend trips to ease our need for traveling, but now I was ready for a real, months-long vacation that would take me away from all this stress and back into my true aspirations. I wanted to finish that book and start doing something that I could handle on my computer while sipping espressos on a Tuscan Villa or mimosas on the Maldives.

Yahir was seeing my frustration and how I'd screwed up my priorities, so he was on board. Money wasn't an issue in this scenario because I had done my due diligence saving up all the points I could. We had enough to redeem for business class tickets around the world plus stay in suites while paying only taxes and fees for an entire month. Maybe our savings could cover the daily expenses and add a couple more paid months. The turning point was that I wasn't ready to repeat the previous years' experience of leaving for months and then coming back to "real life." I was done with this.

I loved designing and loved my life. There is nothing wrong with doing something you love, but I felt like it wasn't doing it for me anymore. I wanted out of all my jobs/projects/work and truly to give my all to my writing passion. I had achieved my life goal of traveling and now wanted to make it my mission to help other girls do the same. I was ready to take the leap and go full on for my dreams once more.

So, we left. We left on our amazing #araujosworldtour number two, saw the most incredible world wonders from the magical Taj Mahal to the beautiful hidden Ljubljana, and had the time of our lives.

We were less naive than on the first trip, but definitely taking in all the culture and amazing views we could. I started writing again and it felt like things were falling back into place.

This trip, we really went all out. We left our beautiful condo that had been our home for four years, sold everything, and left. I could really feel the freedom once more—the possibility to do anything I wanted. Yahir was feeling the same way.

The real bummer we encountered was coming back. We had planned to stay in Mexico for a month to be close to family and to figure out our next steps. It's funny how you notice certain behaviors faster and easier after you've been disconnected from them for a while.

I'm sure you can relate now that you have started changing your life in 10 minutes a day with the 30-day challenge. Now you can really quickly notice when someone else is judging, is negative, or comments on diet culture issues.

The same thing happened to us upon returning. We had been so disconnected from societal expectations, assumptions, and stereotypes that it was like a bucket of ice-cold water landed on our heads.

At first, it was all the same questions: What do you guys plan on doing now? Where will you live? As planned and budgeted for, we weren't sure. We had a couple of personal projects we had been wrapping our heads around.

I knew for sure that I wasn't going back to work and was focusing on my writing. Yahir was looking into maybe getting new clients back in San Diego. We also were not sure if San Diego was the answer, so we were giving ourselves the time to figure out these details before making any decision. Everything was planned and we were confident in our decisions.

The first week or two of this were met with answers like "OK. That's good. Don't rush." In my mom's case, "OK good, but you guys are going to get jobs soon, right?" After the third week, however, our whole idea behind being there for our families to compensate for being gone for so long was met with a serious "Kendra, you have to think about Yahir. He is not getting any younger. Every day that goes by is going to be harder and harder for him to get a job. Do you guys even have a plan?"

WHAT IS IT THAT YOU FEAR THE MOST "NOT DOING?"

That was it.

Again with the expectations. Again with trying to put us in a box. This further exploded when I said, "I'm not going back to interior design yet. I'm going to focus on my book now." Everyone thought I had lost my mind. I knew it was time to move on. I turned to Yahir, and said, "OK, it's time to leave. They couldn't see us relax for two or three weeks before being on our case about the future."

Making the decision to take a break from the profession I'd been working on for the last eight years and leaving the brand that I'd worked so hard to establish, twice, wasn't only easy for me—it was rather liberating. Not because I didn't enjoy designing, or because I wasn't good at it, but because I understood that I wanted to do more. I could be more. That second trip truly made me realize that my calling to write was beyond creating a source of income. It was something inside of me finally ready to come out.

I was criticized for not calling back clients upon returning and for not wanting to take new projects that could mean a good payday. Even Yahir, as supportive as he has always been, said, "Well, maybe you can just take one?" I was sure in my heart that if I went down that road again, I was going to end up where I was three months before: exhausted, frustrated, with a book half-finished, and banging my head against the wall. I knew in my heart what I had to do and I didn't let anyone keep me from following my own path.

Upon deeper analysis and an incredible live workshop, I realized that the reason I hadn't finished those first writing projects was not only for lack of organization, but for lack of a better motivation.

If you start any project with the sole purpose of making money, you are going to eventually find yourself unhappy and unmotivated.

Maybe you managed to push through and did make the money, but that won't bring you happiness. It's not me saying it. Go ahead and Google the topic. Tons of gurus and experts have something to say about this.

Danielle Laporte said it well in her book *The Desire Map*. She talks about a girl she encountered while giving a conference in a college. This girl was majoring in finance, even though she hated it, because it was good money and what her father wanted. He was paying her tuition. Danielle goes on to say that she foresaw two things in that girl's future: A Mercedes and Prozac.

I finally gave myself the time and was open to truly listen to my heart for my calling, just like I had once done when I was younger and found out that freedom and traveling were what I'd longed for the most. I realized that now, as an adult with some experience in life and some adventures in my past, I really longed to help others fulfill their own dreams.

I was surprised at how passionate and motivated I was at the simple thought of helping others for a living! If you can truly understand what your true passion is, you can make that your job and your lifestyle.

The moment you understand that, and take the time to figure out what your heart is saying beneath the chatter of the mind and outside of anyone's opinion... when you truly close your eyes and envision yourself at the end of your path looking back to this moment with an open mind and an open heart, you can see yourself as you are today in a different light and truly understand what your next move should be.

What is it that you fear the most "not doing?"

When you are clear on that, it becomes clear what you must accomplish in your life and what you need to let go. This is the moment when everything comes together, and you truly understand the purpose of your existence. I cried at how intense this simple exercise was.

I'm not suggesting you leave your job just yet. Simply be open and ready to take the next step toward the life you truly desire.

You know better now than to settle for what is "normal."

You've spent the last 30 days working on yourself: improving your self-esteem, learning to accept your outer self as much as your inner self. You know that you are a #badass queen worthy of your dreams and that they can be yours if you put in the time. You are grateful for everything that you have today.

You have an amazing relationship with yourself and will never again stand for anyone who is trying to bring you down. You have come a long way since the judgmental girl that started reading this book and have now blossomed into a confident

#girlboss of your own life ready to make the changes that will lead you to living the life of your dreams while ignoring what anyone thinks of you, regardless of who it is. You can't read other people's minds anyways.

We've worked on laying the foundation. Now it's time to start building that amazing life that is true to you and that is in complete alignment with your heart and your soul.

You are about to discover your true purpose in life and what moves you to do the things that you do. We are going to go over what has been stopping you from accomplishing it in the first place. We'll tackle head-on those roadblocks so you can move forward on your path to a life lived fully on YOUR terms and not anyone else's.

INDIA

LJUBLJANA

CHAPTER 7

What Do YOU Really Want?

Keyword: "YOU"

I want to start by congratulating you, Girl! You are such a #badass for coming this far in your transformation to the ultimate and truest you that you could possibly imagine!!

YOU DESERVE A TOAST. Rest assured that I'm toasting to you right now!!

Before we go into full-on planning mode and discovering exactly what your life will look like a short 30 days from now, I want to go over what goes on in our minds and hearts every time we hear the words "goal," "achievement," "planning," etc.

WHOSE GOALS ARE WE CHASING?

During our entire lives, we have been programmed to follow rules and to follow standards, to "not color outside the lines." We have also been taught that goals are about achieving something bigger than we've achieved before, about proving that we can, about being disciplined and about hustling.

Whose goals are we chasing?

- A million dollars
- Launching a business
- A vacation in Bali
- A new designer handbag
- A pair of Louboutin's AMAZING stilettos
- The perfect body
- 1 million followers
- Getting a good paying job, a house, marriage, kids…

While there is absolutely nothing wrong with any of these goals, I have to question what is behind the decision to choosing any of these or their likes as #lifegoals.

- What are we really chasing?
- What is it about the million dollars that moves you to climb every mountain on the way?

- What is it about the idea of a perfect marriage, plus house, plus kids that makes any girl wish for Prince Charming?
- Why love the red-sole stilettos or the Fendi bag?
- Why crave the perfect so-called "bikini-body?"

Kendra, come on! Is all about HAPPINESS of course. Duh!

Most of these decisions are made with our heads leading the way into our idea of success that has been *inceptioned* into our subconscious, like Leo DiCaprio did in the movie "Inception." We've come to a point in our lives when it is time to grow up and set real goals for our lives and become "responsible adults." Many, if not all, of these became the center and drive of our lives.

The more disciplined of us sit down and set goals for ourselves— goals that we think will make us happy. I mean who wouldn't just be happy with a million dollars to buy all the handbags, heels, and as many trips to Bali/Paris/Rome/Thailand as we wanted?

We push for our goals.

We make them our reality in our visualizations. We go as far as to affirm them every day if we are really into them. We tell everyone about them and work our way toward achieving them. There it is... at the end of the rainbow, after all that hustling, and struggles—the gold pot that will just make everything worth it.

- Your parents will be proud and show you off to everyone.
- You will be socially successful.
- You'll get recognition accordingly.
- You'll look at yourself in the mirror and say, "I did it!"
- You will have proven to yourself and to everyone that you can do ANYTHING you set your mind to because you are as #badass as they come!
- You are the role model the world was waiting for!

But...What happens the morning after?

How long does the "happiness" last?

I applaud your for accomplishing whatever you set your mind to! ALWAYS remember that you can, in fact, DO ANYTHING you set your mind to!

I will question once more the ulterior motive behind the goal you so eagerly chose. Of course, happiness is the end goal. All of these are just different paths that lead to the same shiny treasure at the end. I have two questions that I can't get out of my head every time someone shares a goal like the ones above with me:

1. Does this dream make your heart beat so fast that it feels like it is jumping outside your chest every time you talk about it and those around you can't seem to ignore the incredible spark shining on your eyes? or

2. Did you pick this goal because it is "guaranteed" to bring about happiness (according to everyone you know)?

I'm not trying to be a buzz-kill here. I want a million dollars and Louboutin's latest spiked sneakers (mind-blown), however, I have come to understand that there is such a difference as goals made with the head leading the way and those made with the heart leading the way.

That is not the point I'm trying to make. That point will come after. What I'm trying to tell you right now is to question. Question everything you know. Question everything you want. Question why you want it.

- Why one million dollars?
- Why a business?
- Why designer bags and shoes?
- Why the flat stomach and six pack?
- Why traveling?

When you truly sit down and look for the reasons behind it all instead of just focusing on what you think you might get once everything is said and done, it will give you a bigger picture on the truth that is pushing you as well as on how real your expectations are. I heard once that we should always listen before speaking.

Let's take that quote and apply it to goals. How about if you question before choosing?

Own a successful business:

- Do you want to own a successful business because of the joy of being your own boss because your current boss sucks and you can't stand him anymore and can't wait for the day when you don't have to see him EVER again?
- Do you want to be your own boss because you want to be free to make your own decisions and seriously believe you can do it better (aka happiness)?
- Do you want to have a million dollars to feel like you are the queen of the world and can afford just about anything?
- Do you want to have a million dollars because it will specifically mean you can invest/donate into your life's vision or maybe you want to pay for that dream vacation (aka happiness)?

Vacations:

- Do you want to go to Bali because everyone in your feed is going and it looks like the most paradisiac awesome destination in the world? (By the way, it is.)

- Do you want to go to Bali because you watched a documentary on the natives and fell in love with the culture and traditions and are just dying to experience them in person, heavenly massage included (aka happiness)?

Awesome heels and handbag:

- Do you want to have them because of the status re-affirmation it means, and whatever Fendi designed this year is not as important as the logo being visible or the bag looking "high end?"
- Are you after the amazing Italian and French designs because of the quality and, while overpriced, the colors speak to you and make you feel incredibly vibrant and alive to see them in your closet (aka happiness)?

The reason behind your goals, behind your days, behind everything that you do is just as important as the actions themselves. Because we have but a single, limited life, the actions you take every single day and the goals you go after every morning should be aligned and in complete sync with what makes YOUR heart happy.

Do What Makes YOU Happy

Remember that this is a book about designing your very own lifestyle. A Rebel Lifestyle. A life on your terms. Life on your terms, as explained in many different ways through my ramblings in these pages, is as simple as discovering what makes YOU happy and making *that* the center of your life. It's about taking a hard look at what you have set as your life goals and asking yourself, with COMPLETE honesty, "Is this a goal that my heart is screaming at me or have I been predisposed to want this because it corresponds with the illusion of happiness people around me have?"

LIFE ON YOUR TERMS, AS EXPLAINED IN MANY DIFFERENT WAYS THROUGH MY RAMBLINGS IN THESE PAGES, IS AS SIMPLE AS DISCOVERING WHAT MAKES YOU HAPPY AND MAKING THAT THE CENTER OF YOUR LIFE.

The funny thing about happiness is that, for most, it is all about getting there. It's all about finally getting it after walking the path. In reality, happiness should be a part of your everyday life. You don't "achieve" happiness after checking off an item off your bucket list, trust me I've tried.

#happinessisalifestyle

Happiness is something that you feel every single day when you live a life completely aligned with your truth. When every single day is a testimonial of who you truly are and you are chasing dreams that make your heart, not your head, jump up and down. Happiness is a way of looking at life even if those things are not happening because you are living in complete harmony with your soul and with your heart and showcasing your amazing authenticity.

That's it!!

Authenticity.

My goals are not your goals. Nor am I trying to make them yours. Your best friend's goals are not yours either. Your mom's idea of utter happiness is not yours either. Your heart is unique to you and whatever it wants will be unique to you as well.

That doesn't mean that no one else has ever wished for the perfect hubby, but the way you do it, is unique to you. That is

HAPPINESS IS SOMETHING THAT YOU FEEL EVERY SINGLE DAY WHEN YOU LIVE A LIFE COMPLETELY ALIGNED WITH YOUR TRUTH. WHEN EVERY SINGLE DAY IS A TESTIMONIAL OF WHO YOU TRULY ARE AND YOU ARE CHASING DREAMS THAT MAKE YOUR HEART, NOT YOUR HEAD, JUMP UP AND DOWN. HAPPINESS IS A WAY OF LOOKING AT LIFE EVEN IF THOSE THINGS ARE NOT HAPPENING BECAUSE YOU ARE LIVING IN COMPLETE HARMONY WITH YOUR SOUL AND WITH YOUR HEART AND SHOWCASING YOUR AMAZING AUTHENTICITY.

one of the most wonderful and, at the same time, most scary things about this life.

We are unique—each of us. We have things in common with some people, but other things in common with another group of people. In reality, there is no one group that fully conveys all of our different aspects. That is because we are unique.

YOU ARE UNIQUE!

That scares the shit out of you and complicates things.

Why can't you just like the things your mom would want you to like? That would make life so much easier...

There comes a point in your life, mostly likely in high school when you don't want to be the-weirdo-with-the-weird-fetish when all the other girls seem to like football players, even though deep inside you are drooling all over the Sheldon type. You train your brain to like them as well and your whole body believes it. For a second there, you truly do believe you like football players, so you exclusively date them from then on. Life happens and you continue with your adopted crush of football players, until one day you bump into a funny looking, nerdy guy who asks for your number and you kind of get annoyed but at the same time can't help but wonder, "What would it be like?"

He could have been the ONE. He could have made you happier than you ever thought you could feel, but you were not able to see it or to give him an opportunity because a long time ago, in the rough teenage years, you did your best to fit in. As a consequence, you lost your true, authentic, stereotype-defying voice. This is especially true if you never left your hometown or your childhood friends.

Don't worry. I got you!

That most definitely won't be you because we will make sure to unearth whatever it is that you have been burying deep inside your heart. Just like we scratched the surface with your body and your wants, we are going to go even deeper until those wishes, those dreams, and that Sheldon-crush—that is as unique to you as your own personality—come forward and take full command of your life.

The one thing that I want you to take from all of this is that in addition to your goals in life, every single decision that you make from now on should be in complete alignment with your soul, with your heart, and with your real and unique true-to-you happiness!!

Back to the topic of goals that are led by the heart versus goals that are led by the mind. What does it look and feel like when a goal is made with your heart as opposed to a goal that is made with your mind?

Let's go back to our previous example of having your own business. You decide that your goal for the year will be to finally start your own business due to the possibility of financial and time freedom. You imagine yourself conquering the world one sale at a time. Maybe because entrepreneurship is the mainstream idea of success and you believe it's your idea as well. That is your mind talking.

You may picture yourself as the next Arianna Huffington becoming ultra-successful and a millionaire. You may picture yourself as Miley Cyrus, achieving incredible fame on stages around the world to express your message. (Is it just me?)

On the other hand, a goal with heart is a goal that comes from your inner self. Your heart is speaking to you and letting you know what it wants. It's not about numbers or actions. It's about feelings. It's about how you want to feel versus what you need to do.

Have you ever had one of those moments when you feel the need to do something, even though it makes no sense at all? Like when I told my husband that I wanted to leave everything and travel the world for six months. It could be argued that it didn't make a lot of sense financially or career wise; it only made sense for my spirit of adventure.

I knew in my heart, however, that I wanted nothing more than to explore the world; everything else was just secondary. That is a goal led with the heart. It wasn't about anything else except my true self coming into the light and saying to me: "You can be an interior designer all day long and be awesome. Cheers to you. What I really want, however, is adventure and freedom. Do something about it."

So, I did. I decided to give myself that adventure and freedom I was craving. We could take a trip around the world, maybe hit some major spots or maybe some others that were not as touristy. Obviously, I would include my hubby in the planning, and set a date to leave. ;) ;) It was THE BEST decision by far!

See what I did there? It was about feelings first. Then I turned those into actions instead of starting with the actions and hoping for happiness at the end.

Pure happiness all through the process resulted from that one decision. I could hardly hide my smile when telling everyone what we were doing. Even while planning, saving—and on the days that we went through our daily budget by noon and had to stay in for the night—my heart was lit up with joy because I was acting in complete alignment with my truth and with what I really wanted.

It wasn't an acquired dream. It wasn't something I decided to do to prove to anyone that I could do it. It was about being honest with myself about what I wanted out of life, and then doing it. As simple as that. That is why we now travel for months on end. Even when we don't, we take trips monthly. We are now working on a way to make that our permanent lifestyle.

I was brave enough to listen to my heart and create life goals based on what I heard. I didn't care about what anyone would think. I didn't pay attention to what others were expecting of me or of us. I only cared about what my heart was saying. I do it every time my heart says something different.

Just like with dreams and goals, the heart can change. It's OK! You are free to be whomever you want to be, even if that means you are different from who you were 15 minutes ago.

You can be and do anything.

This year, my heart wants me to share this story. It's why I paused my interior design business to focus on writing. Obviously, I'm still traveling, but again, my heart is leading the way.

Why? Because when I act in alignment with my truth, happiness becomes a lifestyle, not a destination or a treasure at the end of an uphill battle. It's part of every day. Even if one day everything felt like crap, you are still happy in the end because you know that you are doing what's right for you.

BECAUSE WHEN I ACT IN ALIGNMENT WITH MY TRUTH, HAPPINESS BECOMES A LIFESTYLE, NOT A DESTINATION OR A TREASURE AT THE END OF AN UPHILL BATTLE. IT'S PART OF EVERY DAY. EVEN IF ONE DAY EVERYTHING FELT LIKE CRAP, YOU ARE STILL HAPPY IN THE END BECAUSE YOU KNOW THAT YOU ARE DOING WHAT'S RIGHT FOR YOU.

Every time I dress in the morning and I find myself struggling, I ask myself, "Who am I dressing for?" I usually struggle when I'm not dressing for myself. Every time I set a goal, I ask myself, "Why is this so important?" If it is about proving something to someone, then it's not the right goal and I will suffer every day I go down that road if I follow through.

Every time I dress for myself, post for myself, chase goals for myself, however, life is amazing and happiness is at every corner. I feel fulfilled even with little things because everything I'm doing is being true to myself.

When you start living your life in alignment with what you truly want, you'll soon realize that you are happier than you ever thought you could be—all because you are following your heart in everything that you do!

This is what living life on your terms is all about. YOU DOING YOU for the sake of you and in spite of you and everyone else around you—friend or foe.

What does your true authentic life look like to you?

Download the free workbook at www.momisnotalwaysright. com/resources and discover what your heart is telling you and how you'll accomplish it in 30 days!

Put down this book and head over to www.momisnotalwaysright. com/resources to download your free copy RIGHT NOW! After you are done, turn to the Challenges section and start Challenge 2 while you are still reading this section! I promised you an action-packed month—I'm delivering!

Are you ready to #designalifeyoulove? Join me in the next chapter!

BALI

BALI

CHAPTER 8

Shining A Light On Your Obstacles

That's it! You finally found your true calling in life! You found your unique dream that is completely aligned with who you truly are and in total sync with your heart's calling! You've come to this point by reading the previous chapters, doing all your exercises and have realized, even though you kind-of always knew, that you are the ultimate shoe lover!

You, with all that blinding confidence that you now exude, decide to switch careers because shoes simply make you happy! They're like music to your ears and you can't get enough of them. The dream is simple: Stop doing what you are doing and open the most awesome shoe store in town! You are going to dress the whole town in the best possible shoes every season. Of course, you get to try on new shoes on a daily basis. You are going to rock this!

You start making your plans and looking at your options—maybe even look for commercial places. The dream is exciting as always, though you soon realize is not as easy as 123. It will require some serious work and maybe even sacrifice. That is OK because it's what your heart truly wants, so you can do this!

You start sharing your newly-found dream and asking for opinions on this and that and start facing good and bad criticism. Your colleagues start questioning your every move since, "You didn't go to school just to start 'selling shoes.'" They find it degrading. At some level, you agree with them.

Your idea of success wasn't really to become a store front owner. I mean, you went to school and got your amazing degree and are respected in society as such; money can be really good. Still, you continue on—still passionate, but a little beaten.

Your family goes back and forth with their opinions on your decision. On one hand, they supported you through school and they aren't really sure this is the right path. On the other hand, they want to see you fulfilled, so at some level, they support you anyway.

Your best friend even, while really excited for you, asks how you are going to make it happen. Honestly, at this point you still don't know, so you don't know how to answer. An awkward moment arises as you can literally feel the disapproval in her eyes.

You keep pushing. You say to yourself, "This is what I truly want! I'm just going to go for it. I listened to my heart and it screamed at me: SHOES!! So, this is it." As the days go by, starting a business seems a little harder than expected. You start to question yourself, "Why am I doing this? I'm doing well now. What more am I looking for? Why bother? I made someone of myself already and I'm making it. Why change that?"

Slowly, day by day, the initial fire you started with slowly starts to fade away, and long gone are the days of reaffirming your purpose to yourself and talking to your tribe about your deepest desires. All the while, challenges keep presenting themselves. Against everyone's better judgment and your own insecurities, you make it to an online "store opening." You got some good reviews. We all love the shoes, of course, because your taste is awesome, but it isn't exactly what you signed up for.

You are missing the crowd of raving fans coming in floods to buy the shoes and an "online store" wasn't the plan. You wanted a real store, the best shoe store in town, mainly to prove everyone wrong. "Online stores are fake," you think. "You couldn't even make it to a real-life storefront. You are fake in all of this. Everyone was probably right..."

After a few days and a lot of struggle, "real life" settles in. This was an awesome adventure, but everyone is still against it and you're not making the thousands of dollars you thought you were going to make in the first month.

Between pushing harder or calling it, you go for the latter. It's the easier bet. Maybe your heart can want something else, though you know you probably won't ask again. You pack up your bruised ego, put the inventory you have on clearance, and move on with your life. At least you tried.

A year goes by and you continue life as usual. Before you know it, five years have gone by and you are pretty satisfied with your life. When you are completely honest with yourself, though, you know deep down that you are not 100% fulfilled. You are not living your WOW life. You are content and most days you feel honestly happy, but you know what WOW feels like and it's not this.

You felt it for a few weeks when you were pursuing your shoe store dream, when you were acting in complete alignment with your true desires, when you were going through catalogs, online business plans, website design, and every time you talked about it, there was a light shining through you, a light that you haven't seen in a long time.

One day, one of your colleagues—the one who criticized you the most when you wanted to leave your practice—tells you she is just starting a new side hustle based on her children's new interests and will quit her existing career. She is beyond excited with this new adventure that will bring her closer to her kids and you can see her glow! You see that light once again—the one you saw on your own eyes a few years back.

You are honestly happy to see her so fulfilled and you cheer her on! Deep down it hurts that she couldn't be that supportive of your dream, but you are a true friend and you do what she couldn't do for you. While she is rambling about all her plans you start thinking, "What stopped me?"

You curse yourself for ever letting everyone get in your head, for giving in to your insecurities, and for giving up so easily. You admire her for not giving a damn. That could've been you. So you go home, pour yourself a glass of wine and say, "I'm doing just fine!"... but deep down, you know that is only half true.

The Different Faces of Fear

The real reason anyone stops pursuing his or her dreams and gives in to "the easy path" is fear. No need to sugarcoat it. It's always fear. Fear is behind every single decision we make that goes against our true nature and in favor of not disrupting the status quo.

It is a crippling fear that stops us from opening the most wonderful shoe store, or traveling the world, or finally telling our mom that her dreams are not ours. Fear.

THE REAL REASON ANYONE STOPS PURSUING HIS OR HER DREAMS AND GIVES IN TO "THE EASY PATH" IS FEAR. NO NEED TO SUGARCOAT IT. IT'S ALWAYS FEAR. FEAR IS BEHIND EVERY SINGLE DECISION WE MAKE THAT GOES AGAINST OUR TRUE NATURE AND IN FAVOR OF NOT DISRUPTING THE STATUS QUO.

Fear is sneaky though. Fear can take many forms and be disguised as many things that will hurt you, paralyze you, and actively stop you from conquering it and achieving your deepest dreams. Fear is not the enemy, though. Fear is simply a sign. Fear is literally the body's response to the unknown.

Imagination is a tricky bitch. It can come up with the most horrific outcome for anything and everything that you are about to do. That horrific image produces fear in you. The fear will be as big as the image was threatening. That fear makes you stop, second guess yourself, and doubt everything you know which is why is so important to recognize the fear in whatever form it comes. Fear is a sign that we are on the right track. Instead of fighting it, we can use it to fuel our ambition.

"I'm too busy. I don't have time."

"I can't afford that."

"Why bother?"

"What will people say?"

"It's not what my parents expect of me."

"I have responsibilities."

"Who am I to defy society and do something different?"

"All of my friends are doing it."

"Who do I think I am?"

All of these are faces of fear. There are many more. We will tackle each one individually. I will give you real-life tools to recognize them as they appear and to transform them into fuel instead of water for your fire. You've come a long way from the second-guessing, insecure girl you were a month ago. You have become a strong, #badass girl who knows her self-worth and knows exactly what she wants her life to look like.

I've given you the tools to create the most amazing relationship with yourself, to make yourself a priority in your own life, to create the stepping stone to facing everything and everyone around you, and to "come out" as your true self instead of a people-pleasing "nice girl."

Now, I'm going to give you the tools to create the life of your dreams actively and to overcome any fear that comes along the way by transforming it into your drive and keeping your head up high.

My Fears

After I went through the process of discovering what my true calling was, similar to the one you experienced in Chapter 7, I settled on writing a book about how I had somehow broken the mold that time and time again I was being forced to fit into. I truly felt that I could help someone get the courage to do the same.

Deep inside of me, I felt happy and called to help other girls not fall into the trap of societal expectations. I FELT extremely excited about the realization that I could be an author and actually help other girls who have been through what I have to understand their full potential, love themselves, and pursue their dreams in spite of what other people think!

The process started flowing. I sat down and started making a plan, researching how-to, what not to do, and started writing. Halfway through my planning, it dawned on me: I was going to write a book that EVERYONE was going to be able to read. I felt exposed and embarrassed-in-advance and I started to feel it.

Who am I to tell people how to live their lives? I don't have a near-death experience to tell... well except for the time we got too drunk in Oaxaca and had to trust our new "friends" to get us safe to our AirBnB (sorry, Mom)... but that wasn't life changing.

Nothing extremely bad has ever happened to me. I've never been in a car accident or been abused and rose from the ashes with new-found glory. Nothing truly horrific and life changing has ever happened to me. All I've ever done was rebel against my mom's best wishes and follow my heart instead.

People are going to think I'm an idiot. I started thinking about everyone I knew from elementary school classmates to people I met at a party once. I don't talk to these people EVER. I don't even log into my Facebook anymore; however, in the midst of a life-changing decision, the fear disguised as insecurity came crawling in. "What if this is a total failure? Everyone will know..."

I felt self-centered and dumb for trying to pose as an "expert" when in reality I had just caused my parents headaches while growing up and into my adulthood. Then I realized fear and insecurity were not something I experience often. They were new to me at this deep level. I'm the kind of person who makes up her mind and picks up the phone to call whomever can help.

That is how I've gotten clients for my design business fresh out of school with no previous experience. That is how I became a university teacher at 24. That is how I got my amazing flexible job at my favorite furniture store in the world and then became a manager. I just literally picked up the phone and asked if they needed help, no hesitation. #truestory

I'm not the self-doubting, victim type. I say to myself how beautiful I look every day. I take control and find a way out, in, through, or past anything that gets in the way. I love myself SO much and know I can do anything I set my mind to because I've done it, time and time again, both personally and professionally.

I've been to 35 countries just on a whim! Why was I experiencing these deep insecurities? I realized I was going through this mental hell because it finally meant something bigger. Something true. I had openly listened to my heart and asked for my purpose and it had responded.

This meant that the stakes were higher. It wasn't just rejection; it meant failing at my life's purpose while everyone watched. I experienced the biggest fear and self-doubt in my life when it was time to go after what my heart truly wanted the most. I learned that the bigger the fear you feel, the more authentic and true the dream is.

So, I faced it. I remember everything I learned in my 30 years on earth and looked at fear in the eye and said, "Fuck off!"

How? By changing the narrative.

It's all in our heads!! I had full control! Instead of focusing on the fear I had of failure/success/embarrassment/all of the above, I switched that to the fear of not doing it. What would not accomplishing this dream mean? I pictured myself at the end of my life, with a ton more trips under my belt, wondering what it would have been like to dedicate my life to empowering women.

That was scarier than the thought of making a fool of myself. The fear of not having the balls to go through with it. So, I used that fear instead to push me through every sleepless night, every lazy day, to reaffirm my WHY, and to come out victorious.

Did the fear ever leave? Never. Did it substantially diminish? You bet your sweet, perfect ass it did! I chose what to focus on and I chose myself. I chose my heart and my dreams over the horrific images my imagination threw at me that resulted in fear. What you focus on expands. I chose to focus on my purpose and my calling and that pushed me through the finish line.

HOW IS FEAR SHOWING UP IN YOUR LIFE?

How is Fear Showing Up in Your Life?

Girl, at this point there is no lying to you. It's fear stopping you. You know it. I know it. Some outsiders peeking into your life know it. Everyone trying to achieve his or dreams knows it. So, how do you move forward from this paralyzing fear and make it to your magical dream life?

Identify exactly how fear is showing up in your life and remove it. YES, it's as simple as that. This is not about an intricate plan to dismantle fear and attack it like it's the enemy because it doesn't have to be. On the contrary, it's about turning fear into your ally; that way you'll conquer it.

Like I told you before, it doesn't go away, but you can have the tools to work with it instead of against it, and make it all the way to the finish line. Let's face it, who wants to waste precious energy fighting fear when you have a lot of hustling to do and a life to live to the fullest? Not me and definitely not you!

In order to do this, we need to identify what mask fear is wearing in your life. The mask will be the excuses you are using to tell yourself that you actually CAN'T have that thing you dream about. It can be anything from fear of failure to "I don't have enough money."

Those are excuses our fear creates in our heads to make us stop and not move forward. I get it. Fear is actually built into our subconscious for a reason. It is meant to keep you alive, however, when we are talking about achieving your goals and deepest dreams, it is only stopping you, not really saving your life.

How is fear showing up in your life?

Let's do a quick exercise. Grab a piece of paper and a pen. (YES, OLD SCHOOL because it truly works better! If you absolutely can't fathom that, use your notes app or something similar.)

Take a deep breath.

Write at the top of the page what your dream is and draw a circle around it.

Set the clock for 5 minutes.

During that time, write all the reasons you CAN'T accomplish it.

Write absolutely everything that comes to your mind. This is a brain dump experiment. No filters. No erasing. Just write.

Get it all out of your head. Write everything, no matter how silly.

We need to know what is stopping us if we are to face it.

GO ahead. Do it. Right now. Close the book and do it!

Did you do it? Good.

Now take a hard look at what you wrote.

Is there a particular theme?

What did you find out about yourself?

Maybe you wrote something you didn't expect, or maybe you wrote exactly what you knew all along.

YOU, YOUR DESIRES, AND YOUR ASPIRATIONS ARE PERFECT. YOU ARE WORTHY OF YOUR DREAMS. YOU ARE WORTHY OF THE LIFE YOU IMAGINE. YOU ARE WORTHY OF LIVING LIFE ON YOUR OWN TERMS. YOU ARE WORTHY OF LOVING YOUR BODY AS IT IS. YOU ARE WORTHY OF BEING DIFFERENT. YOU CAN BE THE CHANGE YOU WANT TO SEE IN THE WORLD.

Did you run out of reasons before the time was up? Could you have used more time?

What is behind your list? Is it a who? A why? A what? Look at everything you wrote and find what is your biggest and most painful reason stopping you from living the life you want to live.

Let's figure it out to be able to turn that fear into drive.

Remove it by facing it.

DO it!

You are Worthy

Now that you know how you truly feel and what you want your life to look like, you may also start experiencing deep, aching fear. That is a good sign! That means you are on the right path! If your dream is not scaring the crap out of you right now, you may need to dig deeper! In any case, the "Impostor Syndrome" will come knocking on your door. You must remember everything you've learned so far.

You, your desires, and your aspirations are perfect.

You are worthy of your dreams.

You are worthy of the life you imagine.

You are worthy of living life on your own terms.

You are worthy of loving your body as it is.

You are worthy of being different.

You can be the change you want to see in the world.

So, let go. Let go of anything that is holding you back—the insecurities, the guilt, the fear, the doubts. Change the narrative in your head. Take back your control. Understand once and for all that you can have a life truly lived by *your* rules. You can become a rebel against everyone who doesn't agree with you and achieve your full potential while creating the life you were meant to live.

You owe it to yourself and you owe it to those around you. If you live your life to the fullest and shine as brightly as you can, while some will feel overshadowed, others will want to shine as well. You will give them permission to be their true selves and to go after their dreams as well. Who is looking up to you?

If you haven't yet, go straight to Chapter 16 in the Challenges section and start Challenge 2. Start creating your plan and start your life-changing challenge while you keep reading the book! Build on this momentum and put an end to your current life to fulfill the one you were meant to live!

OAXACA

OAXACA

CHAPTER 9

Roadblock #1 – Time

"I want to—I just don't have the time."

That phrase can just kill my good mood in a second, especially when it's coming from a smart, strong, and big-dream girl who just spent the last 15 minutes talking to me about her goals and aspirations.

Seriously?

I understand that life is messy. Some days are honestly bad and you need to pull all-nighters to meet a deadline. Other days, you have more than enough time to binge-watch the last season of "How I Met Your Mother" again (...even though the ending sucks). I am a firm believer that if you want it, you can have it. You just simply need to put in the time.

Nothing will change if you don't start doing things differently. I've been on both ends of this equation. I've made plans and done nothing about them. Obviously, nothing happened except that when I remembered them, I got annoyed at myself for not pushing through. I've also been at the other end: I've made plans, scheduled the time for them, and lived to tell the happy ending! Trust me on this, the second outcome is better.

THE TRUTH IS, TIME WILL PASS YOU BY WHETHER YOU MADE AMAZING PROGRESS IN YOUR LIFE OR JUST SAT THERE AND WATCHED IT GO BY.

The truth is, time will pass you by whether you made amazing progress in your life or just sat there and watched it go by. It's like when you make a New Year's Resolution to travel more this year and then you realize it's April and you haven't even been to the wineries 30 minutes from your house. This is because you failed to plan accordingly and because you didn't have a strong WHY pushing you toward the finish line.

That is not going to be you this time!

At this point, you have sat down, brainstormed your way to dreamland and back, and have a refreshing action plan to transform your life into the one you only dreamed of and is lived according to your rules. You have the strongest WHY of all!

You know exactly what you want. You are not afraid to embrace it and accept it anymore! You know what life following the status quo feels like and you are not having any more of it! Your dream life is waiting for you!

This can be anything from moving out of your current toxic-roommate situation, calling it quits with the beau, getting engaged, switching careers, changing your entire fashion style, giving up bras, starting a business based on your passion projects, moving to the other side of the world, taking a vacation, or simply changing how you show up every day to be your most authentic self. The rest of the decisions will follow.

Whatever your dream life looks like, you know that is in complete alignment with what your heart wants and what your inner goddess is telling you to do, so you can let her out and become your true self. If you feel that time is a major obstacle on you taking the necessary steps to achieving this dream life, we'll go over my favorite, and proven, time management skills that will get you from point A to point B effectively and enthusiastically! Trust me, you've got time! ;)

Just like we learned on at the beginning of this book, it's time to take responsibility for your life and everything in it. From this moment forward, you are going to own your time and you'll start making decisions that will substantially change your life in 30 days or fewer.

You won't judge your past self for not following through before. You won't judge your present self for no following through on a bad day. Life IS messy. Remember always to give yourself love—never hate.

If one day you realize you can't make the time, it's OK. Don't give yourself a hard time. Relax. Have a glass of wine. Congratulate yourself for the days you did show up and breathe. The only rule is not to let a bad day turn into two bad days. It's that simple. Personally, all I ask of you is don't come back to me and tell me you are not living the life of your dreams because you don't have time.

IF SINGLE MOTHERS WITH TWO JOBS CAN GO BACK TO SCHOOL AND GET A DEGREE, TRUST ME, YOU'VE GOT TIME.

If single mothers with two jobs can go back to school and get a degree, trust me, you've got time. I've had two full time jobs while attempting to write a book and plan a vacation while having enough time to meditate, do yoga, and cook dinner every night. Of all those things, the only project that didn't get finished was the book. I have to say, I did pretty well! Yes, you can make time to achieve any goal you want to without burning yourself out or not sleeping. This is simply about time management and proper scheduling.

I seriously believe I have a minor undiagnosed case of ADD. When I'm not sure what the next step is, my head starts to wander, and I start just doing nothing and wasting time. I go to the kitchen and forget why. I lose my phone walking the eight steps from our kitchen to the bedroom. I tend to waste 30 minute blocks of time every time I reach for my phone to check anything because Instagram was open and I started watching stories only to remember that I had to check the weather 30 minutes ago followed by closing Instagram, forgetting to check the weather again, and opening my e-mail instead—there goes another 30 minutes. My husband calls out on it saying "ya te vi, nomas te estas haciendo wey," meaning "I'm noticing, you are just wasting your time." That'll snap me out of it.

I require structure to get things done which is why I love scheduling my days in the morning or the night before. When

I used to work a 9 – 5 job, I only had two times to get stuff done: in the morning or at night. I sometimes used both and sometimes mixed in the weekends when projects required my full attention. Now that my entire schedule is up to me, I need to clarify when I am going to do what, so I plan my days out each morning. This way, I always know exactly what I'm supposed to do next and that keeps my wandering to a minimum. Even if it means writing down "free time" or scheduling Instagram time and giving myself a full, deserved hour. ;)

Where to Find Time

If it only took you one hour a day to change your entire life, would you fit it in? When? Where?

We are working with the premise that you came down to a daily action plan that requires one hour of your time a day while still accomplishing major progress in 30 days. Where do you find that extra hour in your day to dedicate to building your future?

Let's look at your options and remember to choose the one, or the combination, that resonates with you the most. If you'd rather, create your own tips and tricks to make it work! (Obviously, share with me! #rebellifestyledesign)

Mornings

If you are a morning person, or even if you are not (because it is all in your head—trust me), mornings are a great time to do some creative life-changing work. You are just fresh off your restful night. You are thinking clearly—even if it's after the second cup of coffee. You are ready to change the world in the mornings!

I used to call myself "not a morning person;" for the first 28 years of my life, I was a hardcore night owl. I'll give you my tips on being productive at that time, however, if you know me at all, you know that now I'm an avid Miracle Morning practitioner. This lifestyle change has really helped get my creative juices flowing in the morning! If you haven't read the book, I recommend it 100%! (Full transparency though: my miracle morning doesn't start "before 8 am" as suggested; it starts roughly at around 9 am because nights are awesome and those are my terms.) ;)

The best way to have your mornings became incredibly productive and successful is by making the conscious decision the night before to wake up one and a half hours ahead of time to change your life. Why one and a half hours and not just one hour? Because according to many experts, the fastest and most effective way of waking your brain up, besides coffee of course (#coffeelover over here), is by pumping blood to your brain through exercise.

The very first thing I do in the morning, after my gratitude minutes, is get up from bed, throw my yoga mat on the floor and do some quick sun salutations. This takes me five to seven minutes each morning, but is more than enough to stretch my body, get centered, and be ready to take on the day.

This is the exact same routine I started when deciding to write a book. I'd simply set aside one and a half hours in the mornings for yoga, Miracle Morning, and writing before having to go to work and starting "real life." Extra points when my hubby was still asleep since I got all the house quiet just for myself. I made great progress following this routine.

The minute I stopped respecting this sacred time, because "I just needed to make a quick call" or "the design just needed a quick tweak" or "one quick email and I'll start writing" or "I'll start writing again on Monday; this week I need to concentrate on this project" was the moment that book never got finished. That is why I'm adamant about scheduling and establishing your big strong WHY and not letting one bad day turn into two. I've been there and it is the easiest way to let life get in the way of your dreams.

It is also extremely helpful to make a plan the day before on exactly what you are going to get up and do the following day. When you have a clear plan on what you are actually getting up to do, it's way easier to avoid distractions and the snooze button, but you are a morning person, so that is not your problem. ;)

Afternoons

You are not so much of a morning person, huh? Maybe your only free time is between work and school, or during your lunch break. Maybe after a half-time job. Afternoons can be very productive as well, however, the downside of afternoon is that you may be mentally "done" and you are not ready to start a new project in the middle of the day. What you need is the right "mindset routine" to get you aligned with your goals so you can conquer the last hours of daylight being ultra-productive.

When I work on a particular goal in the afternoon, I have to get my previous "morning work" out of my head so I can fully concentrate on my new task. For me, it is not as easy as close that window and open the next one to shift my mindset into the new goal. I have to actively get out of my head for a couple of minutes and get re-focused on my why and the importance of my tasks. How do I do this?

Exercise.

Specifically, yoga. I have mentioned before that I practice yoga at different times each day depending on how my day goes.

When I am working on two different projects on the same day, I use yoga as a transition practice.

We are all smart people. When you have already spent five to six hours conquering the world in your morning activities, you can end up tired, with a headache, and wishing for nothing but your PJs—especially if you are having a not-so-great day. It is too early to give up on your day just yet and exercise can be the answer!

I practice 30 minutes of yoga between my activities. This gets me out of my head, into the moment, and fully focused on my body. I stretch, build strength, and stop thinking about everything that happened. I have a few minutes of peace and gratitude. Afterward, I pour myself a tall glass of water, read my goals and my WHYs, and get right to it.

If yoga is not your jam, try going for a run, doing Zumba, Pilates, boxing, or whatever gets you going. Make sure to concentrate fully on that activity, get fully out of your head, and stop the mental repeating of the morning.

I can't emphasize enough how much exercising in the middle of the day can help you mentally disconnect from your daily activities and get you fresh again for the rest of the day. Even if you are not going to work on your goals that afternoon, but can't seem to get that bad morning off your head, exercise can get you mindful of the present, give you that quick reality escape that you crave, and the happiness boost that you need while giving your body some love after all that stress!

Afternoons can be great for achieving your major goals! I still recommend starting your day with scheduling how much time you'll dedicate to this goal and exactly when and where. By blocking time within the day, whether in the morning, night, or afternoon, having a clear idea of when you'll work on your big goal can help you treat that blocked time as sacred. Never break it—no matter how tempting it is! You'll only regret it later. Trust me on this one.

Evenings.

Oh, my beautiful night owls! My crew for life! Even though I now do most of my work in the mornings, I can still pull an all-nighter like I've never ever stopped when the due date is near. You can accuse me of anything in this world but being irresponsible. I have definitely had sleepless nights working on projects. Damn if those aren't some of the best times I remember from college and interior design in general!

When you have all your day busy, your only time to schedule some "me time" is at night. That is perfectly fine!! Trust me, you can be very productive at night and I admire you and respect you! Yes, you can! Never let anyone tell you that you need to wake up earlier to do things. If you can do them through the night, then that is your time. You can make anything happen. It's like the numbers on the clock don't mean anything! Just remember not to overdo yourself daily and to get enough rest.

To have a night that is ultra-productive, you also need to get in the right mood for night work. Have a mindset routine just like in the mornings and afternoons. I used to get home after a long day at work with interior design projects to finish. The first thing I would do is spend a good hour in the kitchen cooking dinner. I love to cook!! For me, cooking is like therapy.

Just like exercise, an activity that can get you out of your head and relaxed for the next hour of intense work can really help you get aligned with your purpose, in the right mood, and get your inner goddess ready to go. Find that activity that really brings you peace, disconnects you from the day, and gets you back in your zone. It could be taking a long warm bath, meditating, gardening, cleaning, or even exercising. Always, always, recite your WHY.

After that, you'll be ready to dive right into your goals for a good hour with the right mindset. Now, again, make sure you set a specific time for your night goals. Block out time just for these two activities: right-mindset activity and the actual goal-getting. Treat this blocked out time as your sacred time! It will take you at least one and a half hours to accomplish the life of your dreams and beyond. You can even throw in a glass of wine; you deserve it after hustling all day. ;)

No Time? Get Creative!

Are you one of those girls that after reading the three choices above are still thinking, "I have all that time taken already. What else do you have?" I do have more options for you! We just need to get creative and find times when you can work on yourself no matter how little time it is or how busy you are. Any amount of progress you take will be a step forward in the right direction. As long as you don't stop, you'll get there.

What about on the weekends? If your weekday is incredibly packed, you can always do some creative and life-changing work on the weekends. Give yourself Saturday or Sunday mornings to focus on your work, blocking out a three to four-hour window. In this case, still start with a mindset-activity like the ones mentioned above, recite your WHY, and get right on it!

Create your weekends-intensive work instead of daily small actions and get that plan going! Girl, you can make your life as beautiful and as magical as you can imagine. You deserve to give yourself the time!

Have you ever been stuck in traffic or taking long train rides on your commute? These are another awesome opportunity to accomplish your goals! If you have a Bluetooth-enabled car, or a Bluetooth headset, you can make calls while commuting to free up time at home. You can also use traffic to listen to podcasts to get you into the mindset you need to accomplish your goals. That way you can get home and get right to it with no need to add an extra activity!

If you are not driving, but rather using Uber, train, or bus, you can get the actual work done while on the road! Grab your headphones, put on your mojo rhythms, and get to work right there! I love classical music on the road or to commuting work. It simply calms me down. Sometimes a nice flashback to my 90s childhood can get me in the right mood and singing along the lyrics at the same time!

How about finding time at work? Let's all be honest here—you check your Instagram, Snapchat, Twitter, and even Facebook far more times than you should at work. How about if you use that time instead to make your big dreams a reality? You could use your lunch break to do some research saving you time at home. Maybe you could actually bring some of your daily tasks and do them while grabbing a bite on your break. You are essentially in work mode already. If the day is not going great, you could also use this time to read a good book or go for a quick walk to help get you stress-free before finishing up your work day and easing you up for when you do get home.

The truth is, nothing will change if you don't change. Unfortunately, sometimes we let distractions like social media, binge watching a new show on Netflix, or just browsing Amazon for the right lip color eat up hours of our time. It's most definitely OK to take time to relax and spend it on these activities, but it's NOT OK to do so by sacrificing our "me time."

THE TRUTH IS, NOTHING WILL CHANGE IF YOU DON'T CHANGE.

Regain control of at least one hour of your day and give it to yourself, to your dreams, and to your future. The gossip on social media will still be there. Netflix is not going anywhere either. By putting down the phone for an hour or two, you can make incredible leaps toward the life you dream of.

We have covered specific times when you can fit in your "me time" through the day. Make sure you find the right one that resonates with you the most and schedule it today to start tomorrow. Don't wait until the end of the book. Take a look at your activities for tomorrow and find the time that can be only yours! It's totally OK if you change it afterward—if one day is in the morning and another at night. Only you know your schedule and only you know what works best for you.

Just remember, no matter when it happens, treat your "me time" as sacred and never let anything or anyone get in between you and your dreams. Even if one time you do, never let a bad day turn into two.

The reality behind time as a roadblock is not actually time itself. As you already know, it's always fear. This way of masking fear is only the tip of the iceberg of much deeper fear and insecurities. There is a much deeper reason stopping you from taking control of your life leaving behind expectations and others' opinions, and finally embracing the life you dream of.

We will go over deeper fears in the upcoming chapters, but if time is one of the ways fear is showing up in your life, make sure you don't let it stop you tomorrow from achieving your goals. How? By actively facing it and using it in your favor.

Declare right now that you are NOT GOING to waste any more time being a spectator in your life and that YOU DO in fact have

THE REALITY BEHIND TIME AS A ROADBLOCK IS NOT ACTUALLY TIME ITSELF. AS YOU ALREADY KNOW, IT'S ALWAYS FEAR. THIS WAY OF MASKING FEAR IS ONLY THE TIP OF THE ICEBERG OF MUCH DEEPER FEAR AND INSECURITIES. THERE IS A MUCH DEEPER REASON STOPPING YOU FROM TAKING CONTROL OF YOUR LIFE LEAVING BEHIND EXPECTATIONS AND OTHERS' OPINIONS, AND FINALLY EMBRACING THE LIFE YOU DREAM OF.

time to accommodate your dreams. Don't wait until tomorrow! Start today! Start by organizing your days and setting the time aside you'll need tomorrow to accomplish your dreams. Set yourself up for success by doing that RIGHT NOW. That way, tomorrow you are ready to get going! Do it NOW!

If you haven't already, go to Chapter 16 in the Challenges section at the end of the book and start Challenge 2! Use the hashtag #rebellifestyledesign and we will all cheer you on! Today you start designing a life you love. ☺

BELGIUM

BELGIUM

CHAPTER 10

Roadblock #2 – Money

No money? I get it...

As millennials, we were fed a fantasy that wasn't real anymore when it came to the relationship between getting a degree, hard work, and money. It wasn't just our well-intended parents, but our teachers and our society in general.

We were told to get good grades and earn a degree from the best school possible to land a dream job in which we could be successful if we worked hard enough and we could retire happily. What really happened? The Recession. Granted, they couldn't have predicted that, but it stills feels like we were lied to.

I got the good grades and graduated with the support of my parents from a good university. When it was time to get that dream job, however, it was 2010. We were in the middle of the Recession and there were no openings!

No one was hiring.

Everyone was trying to cut costs, not bring more people in! It was a real thing. It was our time to shine, to grab our piece of the dreamland that we were fed from childhood that our degree would open the doors to. The dream wasn't there.

The previous generation calls it entitled because "we are not willing to start from the bottom," but I wasn't looking to start at the top and be the boss from day one. I had no issues starting from the bottom and working my way up, however, those bottom positions weren't available either. If they were, they were limited and many of us were looking. The demand wasn't meeting the supply.

I heard some people were told they were overqualified for a "bottom position," but that they didn't have enough experience for their degree-matching position either. How could we get the experience if there were no one willing to give it to us?

I remember going to an interview for a sales position. I was told that I couldn't get the job because I didn't have a car and the job required house visits. I said, "I don't have an issue with using public transportation at the beginning. Besides, if you hire me, I'll be able to afford a car." I never got a call back.

What happened? I joined the statistics of college kids not making it right after graduation and moved back in with my parents against my internal #rebel, who was screaming at me not to do it. Since there were no jobs, I created one for myself. I printed some business cards, created a free do-it-yourself (DIY) website, and started knocking on doors as the dream designer people were looking for. I had to get creative with my career and my future or I wouldn't have had one.

When you make up your mind to follow your heart and create your dream life, you can either look at all the things against you or you can look at all the things in your favor. Whichever way you pick will substantially affect the outcome of your days and ultimately of your life. Positivity is a real helper, especially when it comes to money and getting creative about where to find more in spite of debts or being currently broke.

Have you ever heard the story of the original #girlboss? Sophia Amoruso, writer of the best seller *#GIRLBOSS* (I need to finish it, but so far, it's awesome!), is a millionaire and the founder of the online clothing empire Nasty Gal. She was a dumpster diver at 22. She even stated in her book *#GIRLBOSS* that the first thing she sold online was a stolen book.

What about Katy Perry, who you know I adore? "It was five years of living in L.A. with no money, writing bad checks, selling my clothes to make rent, [and] borrowing money," she told *Seventeen* magazine.

When I wanted to travel the world, Yahir and I had clients and jobs and a savings account; however, we weren't just about to spend it all on a trip. I mean, as opposed to what my mom sometimes thinks, I do plan responsibly, even when I'm about to say, "F* this shit," to everything and go traveling for months on end.

I did my due diligence and discovered points and miles. They've made all of our trips far more affordable, more lengthy, and way more luxurious than we could've imagined, all without having to come back with an empty bank account. Like our second #araujosworldtour where we stayed only in suites and traveled on business class exclusively on points and miles!

When there's a will, there's a way. Even if the way is telling you to work harder or find another dream. You could be up to your neck in student loans, or credit card debt—because who doesn't love shopping—or you could be debt-free but with no credit whatsoever. You may be neither and be awesome at personal finances! I hate owing money, but I also love spending. Whatever your situation is, there are ways to find money even if you think there are none.

Remember that money as a roadblock for achieving your dreams is a way of fear manifesting in your life and letting you know that you CAN'T do it. Let's go deeper into how to turn the narrative in your head and use that fear in your favor to achieve your dream life.

Do You Really Need A Lot of Money?

Let's talk "dream life." What is it like for you? Did you realize after the exercises in the workbook that it involves going back to school? Maybe it's more about starting your own business or changing your current business. Maybe it starts with simply quitting your current soul-sucking job? Could it be moving to a beach town and starting from scratch or traveling the world? Updating your wardrobe to one that better reflects your true personality?

I get it, everything costs money, but before you start giving up on your truest life dream on account of money, take the time to realize exactly how much you need, at what stage of the process you need it, and what options you have. Keep in mind that putting lack of money as an excuse not to follow through with your plans has more to do with your fear of changing your current situation than with money itself.

For example, writing this book started as, "I'm going to write a book to make money while helping girls live the life of their dreams." After some research, it turned to "I need *at least* $10,000 to make it to publishing successfully." Yahir, obviously, freaked out.

There was a $2,000 course I was CONVINCED that I needed or else nothing would make sense. Then there was a marketer that I HAD TO HIRE. A business coach too, otherwise how would I know what I was doing? I OBVIOUSLY needed the BEST designer for the cover. What about a publicist? Those are important too, aren't they?

The more I read about writing a book and book publishing, the more money I convinced myself that I needed—especially since I didn't have a huge book deal signed that came with a hefty advance. I actually did the opposite, pretty much "quitting" my job to write this book. Money wasn't flowing in and I had a real budget for all the items mentioned above.

I was looking for an "easy" way to do this, a done-for-you deal, because I was afraid of the process, afraid of failing and afraid of not doing things correctly. The perfectionist in me was not willing to take a DIY approach to this, however, I changed the narrative in my mind. I 180ed my paralyzing fear to an empowering belief. I went from "I need a lot of money or this won't work" to "How can I get this started with the least amount of money?" I used

I WENT FROM "I NEED A LOT OF MONEY OR THIS WON'T WORK" TO "HOW CAN I GET THIS STARTED WITH THE LEAST AMOUNT OF MONEY?"

that fear to help me find a way to achieve this dream without money being an obstacle and returned the power back to me.

Just when I was about to freak out further and convince myself that I was in over my head, I turned to what I had learned over years of meditation. I stopped and took a deep breath (more like 10). Then I said to myself, "Everything will work out. The pieces will fall into place when the time is right. What can I do right now to make this work without spending any money yet?"

The answer hit me in the face like a huge *duh!* "WRITE THE DAMN BOOK FIRST—before hiring anyone!!! Write the book. In the meantime, start shopping around for all the people you think you may need without spending a dime just yet." I downloaded a free copy of *Published* by Chandler Bolt (great book if you want to write a book) and followed the instructions one by one.

FACE YOUR FEAR. BREATHE AND TURN THAT FEAR INTO AN EMPOWERING BELIEF. GO BACK TO THE DREAM AND RECOGNIZE THE FIRST STEPS THAT YOU CAN TAKE RIGHT NOW, WITHOUT ANY MONEY, AND TAKE THEM. START WITH WHAT YOU CAN CONTROL AND DO RIGHT NOW.

That is how I started and continued until finishing the book—the book that you are reading right now. If I had left fear-disguised-as-money get in the way, this book would never have come to light. I would have kept my job and clients, to "save for the book," but never would have gotten around to writing it. As a means to escape, I would have used that saved money on another trip.

Face your fear. Breathe and turn that fear into an empowering belief. Go back to the dream and recognize the first steps that you can take right now, without any money, and take them. Start with what YOU can control and do right now.

Once you start doing what is in your hands, it may be the perfect time to start putting money away in a special "Dream Savings Account" for when you get to a point where you truly need some cash to move forward. Before you get to the point of "Shut up and take my money" to everyone around you (or to strangers on the internet who promise to take care of all your problems and deliver your dream life with a bow), look around your connections and check if there is anyone who can help. Maybe you know someone... who knows someone... who can give you some pointers in your dream's direction. Maybe someone in your online world has already been through what you're wanting to achieve and has some answers for you. Reach out and see how they did it. It never hurts to ask!

I found Chandler Bolt through Hal Elrod's podcast. My way of "asking" for advice was simply listening to what someone else who has been through the process had to say on the topic of book publishing. Hal recommended him and interviewed him on an episode, so I listened. When Chandler offered his *Published* book for free, I downloaded it in a second! Just like that. I now had a roadmap to get my book from my head to published (which is what the book walks you through). It was all for FREE. Just because I was open to suggestions and willing to take advice from people who knew more than I did. More importantly, I was NOT going to let my fear stop me.

Never underestimate the power of connections, the internet, podcasts, free downloads, and free webinars. Grab 'em all and send a Thank You note to the author. I have learned so much about online businesses, book publishing, marketing, Instagram, and everything online-related through free webinars and discovery calls. There really are people out there giving you value and sharing their knowledge with the world through these tools as a way of turning you into a customer who buys into their paid plans, however, you can take advantage of everything that is out for free before you start shelling out any money!

Where to Find Money Now That You Truly Need It

You took all the steps that were within your power without spending a dime and have now come to the point of "I actually need some cash to push this forward." I have to say right now that you have more money than you think you do and we'll find it. I'm not judging if you don't believe that yet because this is a judgment-free zone, however, I am saying "check your mindset." Positive thoughts only ;)

The first thing you can look into is what's happening to that paycheck that is coming in every couple of weeks. Are you saving at all? Taking 10% of your paycheck and setting it aside in the previously mentioned "Dream Savings account" is the surest way to have money to spend on your goals. It doesn't even matter how much this is. It could be anything from $10 to $1,000 or more, however, this is the first step to taking responsibility for your finances and making the right moves aligned with your truth and with your goals. That 10% can be a different percentage, just make sure you ARE setting aside a specific amount each time.

Try it. See how that account starts to grow. Before you know it, you'll have more than enough for what you need. Since I love recommending books, according to the *Magic Money* books by Holly Alexander, if you can also set aside as little as 1% for donation, 1% for debt payment, 1% for guilt-free fun (I love this one ;)) and 1% for taxes if you are an entrepreneur, while being grateful every day for the money you receive, money will start to flow your way like magic.

It could be in ways of great new clients, cashbacks, unexpected freebies, discounts, and beyond. I do it, and WOW is it true. A client who owed me money for six months, and who I had totally let go, sent me a check out of nowhere covering his debt without me asking for it. I wanted to attend an event that cost $1,500. By some miracle, and obviously magic money, ended up only paying $150. Yep, 10% and I got the VIP package too. I can go on and on with examples, or I can just tell you to read the book if you feel like you could use some magic in your life. ;)

What else is happening to your check? Take a look at your spending habits and see if there is money going to monthly payments you are not taking advantage of and can cancel. Maybe you realize that you can have pre-drinks in your house before going to the club, saving you a lot of money once you get there. I don't really like budgeting, it makes me feel in lack instead of in abundance, however, I do understand that when we are talking about making dreams coming true, there is such a thing as priorities. For example, cutting my visits to the mall in half in the spirit of dreams coming true, but still going because that makes me feel in abundance.

Maybe that daily Starbucks isn't as important as you think. If it makes you happy and turns your day around by taking that first sip, then by all means, keep at it. This is about doing things your way; however, if it is a matter of not making your own coffee in the mornings out of lack of time, well maybe use the 5 minutes in the am that you spent in the drive-thru and use them to brew your own at home. Buy a cute Starbucks to-go cup so you can feel like nothing changed. Opt for a locally grown or roasted coffee helping a local business in the process and put those $5-$10 you save daily into your dream account. Think about it, is it really about the coffee or is it because everyone else is doing it?

If after looking really hard at your spending and the money coming in, you still need more money for that amazing trip, business launch, or life-altering move you're about to make, let's look at what you can add to your daily activities to generate more money. You don't necessarily want to cut off all your fun-generating activities from your life. You don't want to feel lack, but you want to add more income.

Have you considered a second job? That can be the fastest way to get more income. I used to put all of the money from my 9 – 5 (minus my 10% guilt-free fun money, because—shoes) into a savings account for traveling and for some "peace of mind." I used the money from my business for everyday spending. There were times when I had to dip into my savings to make ends meet, however, it was a RELIEF to know those were there. I could afford to plan a trip since I had set aside for my dreams in my special savings account.

It doesn't have to be a traditional part-time job either; it could be an online gig. Maybe becoming a digital nomad was your dream to begin with! How can you sell yourself online? (No, I don't mean it like that! LOL.) What can you do that is marketable in the online world? There are pages like upwork.com and others where global entrepreneurs advertise their services for an hourly rate to potential employers. The jobs go from Virtual Assistant to Social Media Management and from Interior Design to Accounting. Literally, any trade that you are in, you can offer for an hourly fee.

Hubby hired a graphic designer off the site to create his website and the demand and supply is very good. The quality of the job was great as well! That is a very cool way to earn money, wherever you are, doing the things that you already know how to do.

If the online world scares you, and you are not sure about getting another job, how about doing some freelancing? When I was in my last semester at school, I was hired by my classmates to do their 3-D renderings for our final project. I've always been a techy and I love it, so I made some extra cash, helped my peers, and was able to support myself during those cold months when no one was hiring me before returning home.

Who can you approach who may be in need of your services? Ask! Never keep it to yourself. Ask and let everyone know that you are freelancing. Post it on social media. You never know who is looking for exactly what you are offering!

Now that we are in the social media theme, how about directly asking for money? I'm sure you've heard of Kickstarter and GoFundMe. These websites allow you to create a project and post it on their site with specific details about it and an amount you need to get it off the ground. Then you share it with everyone you know and ask for donations. This feels tacky? Why are you judging?

The truth is that nobody knows what can happen. If you feel like your project is worth it, which it is because it's your dream, go for it! The worst thing that could happen is that you don't collect enough. Period. That is hardly the end of the world.

Research some amazing projects that have come out of sites like those. For example, I'm in the waiting list for the COOLER cooler, which comes with a blender for frapped mojitos, a speaker, and a charger for my phone. I most definitely was all in to fund that project. I was too late, however, and the project had already closed, but my time will come!!

Those guys didn't think it was awful to ask for money. They knew their project was worth it, that they could find their ideal clients through funding, and have them help them make this utopia of a cooler a reality. They did it! Why can't that be you?

If you are still uncomfortable with the idea, check your mindset again. It means you are worrying about what others may think. We flushed those thoughts down the toilet, remember?

Aside from literally asking for money, you could also do a raffle. You know, an old-school raffle. Decide on a prize, like an iPad or a voice-control speaker, and sell everyone you know a ticket at 10 bucks a piece. Explain what you'll do with the money in a way that makes them feel connected and invested. Start with your loved ones and move on to everyone else until you sold all your tickets and got funds to accomplish your dreams.

Have you heard of points and miles? (LOL, that was a joke.) Credit card companies are so eager to have you as a client that they are literally giving away money for new customers! As you know, I LOVE LOVE LOVE this about them. I use them to my advantage and you can do the same for YOUR dreams.

Maybe that cashback money can be used toward your first investment. Maybe through the cashback you pay off a debt and free up some everyday money to use for dream-building investing. Take into account that a lot of the credit card companies do this because they want you to owe them and make their money back on interest. Don't let them. Use the card only to spend what you can afford and take advantage of them by collecting sign-up bonuses and cashbacks that translate into plain old money in your pocket! Money that will be used for good... most of the time. ;)

Now, completely contradicting my previous advice, you could also charge your dream to a card that will offer an amazing 0% APR or to get a spending bonus like I already mentioned and then transferring the balance to a 0% card. I don't like owing and make a point to pay my cards off in full each month, essentially only using them for points-collecting. Sometimes you need the money, however, and the savings strategy will take longer than you can wait. It could, in a specific, well-thought out plan, work if you spend the money first and then use that 10% you are setting aside for saving or debt payment to pay it off over time.

Against my own advice, I have invested in a business by completely charging the initial payment onto a credit card and have been using the profits from that same business to pay it off each month. I got a credit card with 21 months of 0% APR specifically to do this. I only did this, however, because I actually have the money in my savings to pay back the credit card. I just didn't want to lose my capital like that. I decided to risk it.

The business is coming through, so it has been working, however, I advise against it in 90% of the cases. Debt is addictive. It can take you from charging one thing to charging 100 and only paying the minimum. It will also make you feel like you are drowning in debt, which is the opposite of feeling abundant. It will make you feel like you can't achieve your dreams because you are chained to this debt. I hate feeling stuck because I love to feel free in every aspect, including when it comes to money.

Take a look at the actual investment that you need to make and if you, as a responsible adult, can come up with a payback plan that makes sense. If you have the money but can't really spend it all like that and you are not fooling yourself, then go for it. Just remember to take a look, a second time and a third time before actually hitting BUY.

When it comes to money as a huge roadblock in your path to living the life of your dreams, I need you to do as you have been doing since you started reading this book—be completely honest with yourself. What really is happening in your head or your life that is causing you to think like this? Have you been conditioned by society, family, or culture to fear money? What is really behind this fear? The answers may surprise you.

When you feel that fear creeping in and feel yourself paralyzed over lack of money, go back to what we said before and turn the narrative around by asking, "What can I do right know to come up with the money I need?" Turn the power back to you and you'll look at your options with a sense of possibility instead of a sense of defeat. Then, doors you never even knew were there, will open. That is how we rig the game and make fear our ally instead of our enemy ;)

FLIGHTS

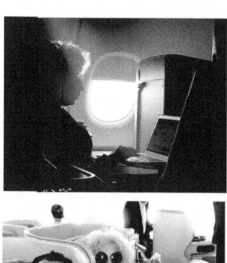

FLIGHTS

CHAPTER 11

Roadblock #3 – Other People

You got up in the morning, did your gratitude exercise, continued with some self-love affirmations in front of the mirror, read your goals, and powered through the morning full of energy and true happiness from all the love you feel for yourself. All of a sudden, someone says something you don't agree with. When asked for your opinion, you don't speak your mind because somewhere inside your brain a little voice comes out from the shadows and says, "What would *they* think?"

It happens to all of us. I am a firm believer of the saying, "If you don't have anything nice to say, don't say anything," however, holding yourself back on account of what others may think goes against your authenticity and your desires to live your truest life.

Letting other people run your life is like saying, "I want to be happy, but only if you agree." We have been conditioned from the start to worry about what other people might or might not say about us and it's hard to break free from that mentality. The truth is, the only way you'll be able to live your truest and happiest life is by following what is in your heart, whatever that may be.

LETTING OTHER PEOPLE RUN YOUR LIFE IS LIKE SAYING, "I WANT TO BE HAPPY, BUT ONLY IF YOU AGREE."

This is a strange concept if up until this point in your life you were great at following the rules and fulfilling expectations. If you are reading this book and got this far, that means that deep inside you know there is a better way. You know deep down that while you may be content with the way things are, you know there are things you want to do, say, or create and you haven't done so because you feared criticism.

How to Overcome It

Let me get completely real with you. The fear of being criticized never goes away. Every time you see someone walking down that street and think, "Wow! She is so sure of herself!" know that she, too, is struggling to ignore others' comments. Even pop stars have these feelings. You know those people that seem not to think about these things have in common? They decided that what they thought of themselves was more important than criticism from someone else.

Remember and make sure to truly internalize Yahir's advice: "You don't read minds." Never. Every time you cover yourself up, don't speak your mind, or don't do what you want, your own mind is sabotaging you by assuming that the things you are insecure about are exactly the things all the people around you are noticing and criticizing.

When we were planning our stop in Dubai, we realized it was going to fall right on our anniversary, so, I wanted to do something special. Now, you have probably heard that Dubai is NOT cheap, but because it was our anniversary, we were OK with splurging a little bit.

The truth is, we almost didn't. When I was looking up special day packages, places to visit, where to have dinner, champagne celebrations, and whatnot, I realized it was not going to come cheap at all. It wasn't the money that almost stopped me from

LET ME GET COMPLETELY REAL WITH YOU. THE FEAR OF BEING CRITICIZED NEVER GOES AWAY. EVERY TIME YOU SEE SOMEONE WALKING DOWN THAT STREET AND THINK, "WOW! SHE IS SO SURE OF HERSELF!" KNOW THAT SHE, TOO, IS STRUGGLING TO IGNORE OTHERS' COMMENTS. EVEN POP STARS HAVE THESE FEELINGS. YOU KNOW THOSE PEOPLE THAT SEEM NOT TO THINK ABOUT THESE THINGS HAVE IN COMMON? THEY DECIDED THAT WHAT THEY THOUGHT OF THEMSELVES WAS MORE IMPORTANT THAN CRITICISM FROM SOMEONE ELSE.

booking, however. It was the idea that the incredible experience was a little too much. A little too "royal treatment" for us like somehow we didn't deserve such an experience. Like we shouldn't do that because that is for "other people" to experience, "better" people...not us.

We were criticizing ourselves for wanting that experience. We were criticizing ourselves for being able to afford that experience as if it were a bad thing.

Upon realizing this, I said, "You know what? This is our anniversary. If we can make it work, why not do it? What if this is the last time we get to visit, or to travel (knock on wood), and we didn't do just what we want?" I booked it!

Off we went to have an amazing day in Dubai with a private chauffer visiting all the famous sites in a day. We went to the top of the highest building in the world: Burj Kalifa. We even had dinner at the only seven-star hotel in the world: Burj Al-Arab. During the day, we truly felt like royalty. It was more luxury than I've ever experienced before. It was a magical day!

Then the next day came and it was time to do what we all do on a trip: share the pictures and videos! This is when things got ugly. We wanted to share, but we didn't want to share. We wanted everyone to see all the beautiful places we'd seen and somehow take them on the trip with us, but at the same time we didn't want to come out as "rubbing it in your face."

The truth is, we were embarrassed to share. Embarrassed of what we had done as if we had done something awful and somehow believed that EVERYONE we knew would criticize us and believe that we were the most show off people in the world.

Then a thought came to my head. "I only believe people are going to feel this way because deep down this is how I feel about what we did." The truth was, we had no idea what other people were going to think. Whatever they thought wouldn't change the amazing time we had.

The idea that we could be criticized, though, would affect something else. Yahir loves to get the "one year ago" reminders on FB. It makes him re-live the moments we've had. He wanted to share those pictures so that one year from today he could look at the memory and smile.

Why would he rob himself of that moment on account of what somebody else would think? Reminding ourselves of this idea, he did it. He posted all the pictures on FB.

Do you know what happened? NOTHING.

We got some likes, some comments, and then the world continued spinning and everybody's lives continued moving forward.

We got our "panties in a bunch" over nothing.

Worrying about what other people think has more to do with what you think and less about what THEY think.

Getting even more honest, most people don't really care about you. I'm not Madonna. More than 99.999% of people in this planet don't care about what I do or don't do—they don't even know I exist! Why would I let the remaining less than 0.001% dictate my actions by assuming I know what they are thinking?

WORRYING ABOUT WHAT OTHER PEOPLE THINK HAS MORE TO DO WITH WHAT YOU THINK AND LESS ABOUT WHAT THEY THINK.

How do you overcome this fear, stop it from paralyzing you, and instead turn it into a drive that motivates you? You have to switch the narrative around and turn the power back to you just like with any other fear. Look at it like this: instead of worrying about what other people will think of you (because you won't know and you can't really control their thoughts), instead think about what you think of yourself.

I'm pretty sure you want to feel good. You want to feel beautiful. You want to feel brave. You want to feel worthy. You want to feel successful. You want to feel all the pretty feelings in the world.

What happens when you don't? When you think you are not beautiful, you feel unworthy of looks. When you think you are not smart enough, you feel like you shouldn't speak you mind. When you think you are not worthy of your dreams, you feel like a fool for going after them.

That is how you change the narrative. By realizing that you control how *you* feel others will perceive you, you bring the power back to you. You, alone, are in control of how you feel. By making those feelings positive, your mind will believe everyone around you is thinking the same way. If you feel pretty, you'll think everyone around you thinks you are pretty. If you feel smart, you'll think everyone around you agrees. If you feel worthy of your dreams, you'll think everyone around you is admiring your efforts.

This is not about fooling yourself. It is about understanding that we have power over our minds and worrying about what other people think is all in our heads. It has nothing to do with them, and everything to do with you.

Set Yourself Up for Success

Girl, you are already winning after our first challenge!! Self-love and self-appreciation are the first steps in setting yourself up for success in the "What will people say?" fear.

It all starts with you. As we have clarified, how you feel and what you think about yourself is what really matters. To make sure positive feelings about you are conquering the ever-popping negative thoughts, you have to continue reminding yourself how awesome you are. You'll continue with your newly-adopted morning routine reminding you that you love yourself for all that you are, just as you are, that everything you want for yourself is attainable, and you are worthy of it.

You may be a pro at doing this at this point, or you may still be struggling with accepting it. In either case, remember that you need to internalize that love and make sure you accept all of who you are. You should be your biggest love story. I said it once and I won't ever stop. You should be your biggest fan and your biggest admirer.

Unfortunately, it is too easy also to become your biggest critic. As we've mentioned, this leads to the "loophole from hell." Be careful and be mindful of what you are thinking and feeling. If you catch yourself having hurtful feelings, maybe feeling guilty about something you said or didn't say, close your eyes, breathe, don't judge yourself, let yourself feel the feeling for about 5 – 10 seconds. Then, open your eyes and see how easy it is to let the feeling go. Next, continue being awesome.

On the other hand, if you catch yourself in the middle of a negative thought about yourself, it is important to remember that you are not every thought you have. Don't judge yourself for the thought. Simply remind yourself that you are a beautiful human being and that you are awesome just as you are. If that feels like a stretch, remember that you are doing your best and move on.

Another awesome way to set yourself up for success is reminding yourself of your WHY—recite it every single day. Make it as visible as possible and make sure never to forget it. Your WHY is your most powerful reason to do what you are doing. It will help motivate you when you are feeling like it is all too much.

Remember why you are doing this. Remind yourself how much your life has changed so far—and how much more incredible it can get—by simply following your heart. Think about how happy you feel now because everything that you do is aligned with who you truly are even if that means ignoring everyone around you. You don't really mind anyway. ;)

Make sure you to remember that everyone you meet is fighting his or her own internal battles. All people do the best they can with what they know and what they have. You are not alone doing this. Make sure to take one step back and practice your compassion. Instead of focusing on what they are thinking about you, find a way to make their days a little better.

Is your coworker always bitching about something? Maybe there is something going on in her life. Next time you see her, compliment her! Tell her how on point her outfit, hair, nails, or last idea was—whatever you can notice. It may not change what she does every day, but you never know how much of a difference you can make in someone's life by being a positive resource. By being selfless about spreading your newly-acquired positivism, you'll feel better about yourself too! Stop second-guessing yourself, and just do it. ;)

If someone criticizes you openly, keep in mind that it has more to do with the critic and whatever he or she is going through, than it has to do with you. Take it as it is. Don't let it affect your path unless it is real, positive, constructive, uplifting criticism from someone who has already been where you are. Even then, make sure it's not just playing into your insecurities.

An amazing and proven step you can take to conquer this fear of being criticized is updating your social media. I have mentioned in the past how important it is to have a tribe who supports and cheers you on your path to self love, self discovery, and living the life you imagine, however, we can't overlook our social media presence.

What do I mean by that? I mean that if you are feeling insecure about what you post because of what will people think, that is a sign that your "online friends" are not serving their purpose, but are playing into your insecurities. How do you break free from this? There is a simple, efficient, and harsh option and there is a subtle option.

In either option, the first step is to realize who is causing you to feel insecure. Are you not posting that awesome picture on Facebook because you are concerned about what your high school friends will think? Is it because you have your entire family as your friends? Is your Instagram now full of the same people you once had on Facebook? Maybe Snapchat for the same reason? Why are these people's opinions so important to you?

As the smart awesome goddess that you are, you already know the answer. It's more about how you perceive yourself than what they think. How do you make your social media work for you?

The subtle option is to go and create a new account with a different email address. Use an alias if you want to and fill it with only positive and uplifting accounts. For example, when I was ready to quit my Facebook after realizing it was too "gossipy" and not serving me at all, I turned to my Instagram account. I had rarely used it before this moment, so I set it up like you would a new account. Instead of "inviting all of my Facebook friends," I started following accounts that were spreading the message I wanted and needed to hear—the one that was lacking in my environment. Messages of self-love, traveling as a lifestyle, body-positivity, travel hackers, couples living on the road, people quitting their jobs and becoming entrepreneurs, more traveling couples, and my favorite authors.

Essentially, I followed people who were living the life I wanted to be living and who were passing along the messages that I felt were true to what I was feeling and what my heart was saying. It wasn't about living vicariously through them; it was about reaffirming to myself that I was on the right path. It was about surrounding myself with the right people who were pushing me to be better, maybe not through direct friendship, but with their posts. I was reminded every day that what I wanted was out there. The life I imagined for myself was real because there were people already living it.

All of a sudden, almost by accident (or maybe maturity), I started noticing the negative people and negative conversations that were happening around me. Now I knew there was a different world out there. I started paying attention to who was talking BS all the time and who was truly interested in other people's goals and pushing them to be better.

It was like removing a blindfold from my eyes and finally seeing people for who they truly were. Some with good vibes, some with negative vibes, some neutral and uninterested. I was able to see who really cared when they asked how I was doing, who just wanted some gossip, and who didn't really care enough to ask. It was a real breakthrough.

This new platform became my online escape. Through it, I was able to grow and to accept myself beyond belief. I also gave myself permission to dream bigger for me and my family and to reaffirm what my heart had been saying all along: "What you want is possible."

I love reading. It has helped me expand my mindset in ways I never thought possible and to learn every day more and more about the possibilities that are out there. This small social media experiment really opened my eyes to my surroundings far more than anything else.

Try this subtle option yourself. No one even needs to know if you don't want them to. Make sure you start surrounding yourself with the messages you need to hear. EVERY SINGLE DAY. This will become your online TRIBE. People who inspire you. People who are defying the status-quo like you want to do. People who are accomplishing their dreams. People who are loving themselves. You can even take it one step forward and engage with these people. Start a conversation and you may even get a friend for life! If you do this, let me know in my Instagram @thekendraaraujo and I'll be happy to engage!

If you are trying to be the best graphic designer in the world while doing all of your work from the road, follow those people who make you think outside the box. If you are trying to be a wedding photographer who creates unique shots, make sure to follow photographers who share the same values as you. They are not your competitors in this life; they are your inspiration! Follow the body positive accounts instead of the "before and after" ones. Follow the dreamers and the doers, not the posers and the haters. Follow accounts that make your heart happy! There is already too much shit going on around you to have it invading your feed as well.

FOLLOW THE DREAMERS AND THE DOERS, NOT THE POSERS AND THE HATERS. FOLLOW ACCOUNTS THAT MAKE YOUR HEART HAPPY! THERE IS ALREADY TOO MUCH SHIT GOING ON AROUND YOU TO HAVE IT INVADING YOUR FEED AS WELL.

You'll soon realize that you'll be able to post happily and freely in this "secret" account without worrying about anyone's opinion! That will give you a self-esteem boost, a chance to be your true self, and maybe even discover who that is! Start sharing your opinions and your values and attracting like-minded people! Start engaging with them! For the love of God, stop checking those negativity-inducing accounts so often!!

This is not about having a split personality. It is about creating a winning atmosphere that may be lacking in your real life. It's about making sure you don't lose sight of your goal, no matter what else is going on around you or what everyone you know is doing. It's great to like your friend's trip to Vegas, but it is far more awesome and uplifting to like and comment on that girl's post who is on the other side of the world and just shared about how she finally published her first book because you want to do the same and can relate to the struggles she is sharing. Try it!

Now comes the harsh option. To be completely honest, it is only harsh in perspective. It is doing everything I've shared in the subtle option, but in your current account. That means doing a deep analysis of your friends and followers and purge your account of everyone and everything that is causing you to feel insecure about yourself and of people who you have no business watching (and vice versa). You do this by either unfollowing them or unfriending them. Why? Because they are not serving you and you are not serving them. Not only are you not serving each other, they are actually crippling your personal growth.

I understand if you may be hesitant about "unfriending" some of the people in your Facebook, Instagram, or Snapchat, however, this is again assuming that you know what they're thinking. They might not care. They might not notice. Even if they do, it just might not even be such a big deal. Truthfully, this is all about you. It's about what you need to thrive. If you need an online escape, then what someone thinks has nothing to do with that. You do what you need to do to make sure you follow your dreams!

My next advice goes hand in hand with purging your social media.

Purge your offline social life cutting communication with all the people who are not serving you. We've been over this as well, but it's time to pay real attention. Who in your life is only there by association? Whose mere presence or negative comments causes you to feel insecure? Do you really need them in your life?

The point here is, that while you work on becoming your best self, and even after you feel you've accomplished it, you have to surround yourself both online and offline with the people who motivate you to do it. You have to, for your own good and to be successful at it.

This means that you start paying attention to how you act and feel around certain people. Who makes you feel positive, accepted, and real? Who doesn't? Based on this, you will start to make decisions about who you are choosing to spend your time with.

This may translate into skipping happy hour with your coworkers because all they do is bitch about everything. Maybe they always

THE POINT HERE IS, THAT WHILE YOU WORK ON BECOMING YOUR BEST SELF, AND EVEN AFTER YOU FEEL YOU'VE ACCOMPLISHED IT, YOU HAVE TO SURROUND YOURSELF BOTH ONLINE AND OFFLINE WITH THE PEOPLE WHO MOTIVATE YOU TO DO IT. YOU HAVE TO, FOR YOUR OWN GOOD AND TO BE SUCCESSFUL AT IT.

make you feel insecure about what you wear, do, or say at the office, which in turn makes you believe you can't be your full authentic self around them. This is a sign that you may need to stay away for a while.

You don't need that in your life, right now or ever.

What about Wednesday night with the girls? Are they all about criticizing each other? Who looked fat in last weekend's event? Who slept with whom? On the contrary, if they are all about helping each other and pushing each other to follow their dreams, by all means, hold them tight and never let them go! That is the tribe I was talking about!!

Do the same with your neighbors, cousins, anyone else in your life you have a relationship with that you can actually stay away from if they are not pushing you to be better. To be honest, do this with everyone in your life. We'll get to how to deal with family in the next chapter.

There Will Always be People with an Opinion

Let me reassure you that the power of the mind is key in the fight with fear when it's presented as other people's opinions. Let's face it, we all want to be liked and no one wants to be criticized. That is just the truth. For some reason, it is rooted within our society to feel that way and to pay attention to what someone else is saying about us. This is why it is so important to understand that the real fight in this "expectations" battle is with how you feel about yourself.

We will dive deeper into YOU being your greatest roadblock in Chapter 13. For now, think about this. No one can hurt you unless you give that person power to. In "accepting your outer self," I told you that if you loved yourself and accepted yourself like the amazing goddess that you are, no critic will hurt you because you'll know your truth and your worth, even if others choose not to see it. If necessary, make sure you re-read that chapter.

The more you stand out from the crowd by not doing what everyone else is doing and doing what is real to you, the more attention you'll receive. The more attention you receive, the more positive and negative comments will come your way. Use them as a sign that you are on the right path! If that opinion is said straight to your face, remember the "Nod and Smile" technique.

You don't need anyone's permission to be happy and to be your true self.

YOU DON'T NEED ANYONE'S PERMISSION TO BE HAPPY AND TO BE YOUR TRUE SELF.

Make sure everything that you do is aligned with what you truly want. Spread nothing but positivity. Do not judge anyone—including yourself. Remind yourself everyday why you are doing what you are doing, how awesome and beautiful you are, and that you are drawing an imaginary line with all those that cause you to doubt yourself. You've got this!

DUBAI

DUBAI

CHAPTER 12

Roadblock #4 – Family

Sometimes—a lot of times—the people who want the best for you, love you to the moon and back, and wish nothing but happiness and success for your life, are also the biggest roadblocks actively stopping you from achieving that same greater success and happiness.

When someone in the world doesn't understand what you are trying to do, that person is bound to stop you from doing it. Truthfully, people are afraid of the unknown. This fear of your parents, brothers, aunts, uncles, or grandparents when you do something different from what they know is so strong. So is their instinct to protect you, even though in the process they might smother you with so much love.

While comments like the following are meant to push you in the path to success, a success they have already accomplished, these comments also fill you with guilt if they are not your heart's calling:

"Continue the family tradition. We are all doctors."

"You have to take over my tutoring business when I retire. Working with kids is awesome!"

"I'll teach you how to take the best pictures so you can be an amazing photographer like me."

The same goes with hints that you are not making them proud with your current life choices.

"When will the wedding come? You are not getting any younger..."

"It's time you grow up and stop traveling so much and start doing something better with your life."

"Honey, you are spending the best days of your life *fat.* Is that what you truly want?"

Guilt-inducing comments produce heartache even when they are meant for you to wake from this "immature" situation they perceive and "get a hold of your life" according to how they think it should look.

That guilt is a B-I-T-C-H. With all capitals and in slow painful motion.

This is the one of the major fears you'll face: the fear of feeling guilty by letting down those who care about you. This one is tricky, let me tell you. The guilt that a mother can so easily, and almost with only a look, induce in you can be so DAMN HURTFUL and strong that you lose sight of the main lesson I've been trying to teach you: it's all about YOU. Yep, even this is about what you think and feel about your decisions and not at all about what they think and feel about them.

Think about it. Think about what we've been talking about for days now. No one can make you feel anything unless you feel it first. If you are 100% sure of your decisions and feel ultimate happiness for making them, then your parents' disapproval might sting a bit (more out of surprise than of constant need for approval), but you'll be able to hang up the phone or walk out the door and still feel fantastic about your choices!

YES!! IT IS POSSIBLE! I PROMISE!

THE GUILT THAT A MOTHER CAN SO EASILY, AND ALMOST WITH ONLY A LOOK, INDUCE IN YOU CAN BE SO DAMN HURTFUL AND STRONG THAT YOU LOSE SIGHT OF THE MAIN LESSON I'VE BEEN TRYING TO TEACH YOU: IT'S ALL ABOUT YOU. YEP, EVEN THIS IS ABOUT WHAT YOU THINK AND FEEL ABOUT YOUR DECISIONS AND NOT AT ALL ABOUT WHAT THEY THINK AND FEEL ABOUT THEM.

Breaking Free from YOUR OWN Judgment

Darling, after so many pages, it's time you make the ultimate choice. Are you going to fulfill your dreams and live the life of your dreams or are you going to try to make everyone else around you happy, even if it means sacrificing your truth?

For you to break free from guilt induced by loved ones with your best intentions in mind, you first need to understand that you are not doing anything wrong. Let me repeat: You are not doing anything wrong. It may feel like you are at the moment, but you are not.

FOR YOU TO BREAK FREE FROM GUILT INDUCED BY LOVED ONES WITH YOUR BEST INTENTIONS IN MIND, YOU FIRST NEED TO UNDERSTAND THAT YOU ARE NOT DOING ANYTHING WRONG. LET ME REPEAT: YOU ARE NOT DOING ANYTHING WRONG.

If all you are doing is following your heart, your deepest dreams, and fulfilling your life's greatest goals, you are not doing anything wrong. If you are still single, you are not doing anything wrong. If you don't want to get married, now or ever, you are not doing anything wrong. If you want to quit law school because it robs you of your happiness and want to pursue stage acting, you are not doing anything wrong. If you want to quit your soul-sucking high-paying job to open your own clothing boutique, you are not doing anything wrong. If you want to move to the other side of the country to live in the biggest city on earth even though you'll be away from family, you are not doing anything wrong. If you want to move halfway around the world to a huge piece of land where you can grow your own food, you are not doing anything wrong. If you don't want to follow your family's tradition because your calling is elsewhere, you are not doing anything wrong. If you want to leave everything—career, friends, security—and go travel the world with no return plan, you are not doing anything wrong. If you stop following everyone's advice and instead sit down with yourself to discover what you truly want for your life, and do that instead, you are not doing anything wrong.

It's OK to be a little selfish if it means your happiness and your future are on the line. The guilt that you feel comes primarily from the fact that you haven't fully accepted this. You start

IT'S OK TO BE A LITTLE SELFISH IF IT MEANS YOUR HAPPINESS AND YOUR FUTURE ARE ON THE LINE.

feeling like the most selfish girl on this planet for not helping out, or for staying home, or for not following in their footsteps, or for not having the perfect family, or for simply ignoring their advice. I mean what a bitch, right? WRONG!

You need to take a good hard look in the mirror and start understanding what you are truly feeling. It is a mix of guilt, rebellion, unhappiness, "why can't they understand?" You are probably fighting them by default... Let's try something different.

Close your eyes. Feel those feelings—really feel them and let them invade you without fighting them or justifying your actions. Just let them be. Breathe. For about one minute, breathe and feel them. Don't try to control them. Simply let them exist while you focus on breathing. Then, open your eyes and feel how they start disappearing slowly. This is not some woo woo trick.

The easiest way to fight any fear is to face it instead of running away from it. Allow yourself to face all of this and then watch

YOUR FAMILY WANTS WHAT'S BEST FOR YOU. DON'T DOUBT THAT FOR EVEN A SECOND. THEIR ADVICE TO DO SOMETHING DIFFERENT OR YOU'RE "RUINING YOUR LIFE" BY GOING AGAINST THE NORM COMES FROM A PLACE OF FEAR THAT YOU MIGHT GET HURT, BROKEN, PREGNANT, NOT PREGNANT, END UP ALONE, OR REGRET IT.

it all disappear—almost by magic—after you have given it time to exist. If you need to cry, cry. If you need to scream, scream. If you need to go for a run, go. Do whatever you need to do without fighting the feelings so they can completely dissolve afterward on their own.

Then, read your WHY out loud. Look yourself in the eyes and replace those negative feelings for feelings of happiness from how much clarity you have now and how exciting it is to know exactly what you want out of life instead of just going through the motions. Now let those feelings fill you with such a strong joy that you can't possibly conceive giving them up for anything or anyone. Grab hold of those ideas and feelings. Make them your force every day and after each family visit or phone call.

The better a person you become, the more fulfilled a life you live, the more you give permission to those around you— especially those you love—to be better themselves. You have the responsibility to raise the bar because you can see that it is not working for you as it is. Do what you need to do to make yourself whole. Your loved ones will strive to do it as well based on your example. Don't let this be your end goal. Everyone has his or her own learning curve. We don't judge anyone for not living life a certain way. All people are entitled to living their lives however they please. Remember if you want not to be judged, you must not judge.

Your family wants what's best for you. Don't doubt that for even a second. Their advice to do something different or you're "ruining your life" by going against the norm comes from a place of fear that you might get hurt, broken, pregnant, not pregnant, end up alone, or regret it.

There is a Mexican saying "Mas sabe el diablo por viejo, que por diablo" meaning that they know better because they are older and have been through a whole lot more, not just because they're your parents. In A LOT of things, they do. Even so, that doesn't mean that you don't know what's best for you. The only one with direct access to your authenticity is you.

Take their advice on what's better according to their years of experience and apply it in a way that fits your dreams. For example, if your mom says, "You can't just drop out of college. You won't make any money as a hand-made jewelry seller," she is trying to say is that you need to think further ahead to have something to fall back on if it fails. Apply it by going on with your plans of creating and selling your own jewelry and devise a plan B. For example, start a job at a jewelry store to see how the business works, gain massive insight while also having a steady income to support you and to invest in your own business. You can stay in school so that degree becomes your plan B while going all in with your dream on the side. Do whatever feels most aligned with you.

Do you see what I mean? Understand what they are saying and find a way to leverage the wisdom they give you in a way that works for you. You need to see past their fear that you are making a mistake and will regret it later. Seek to understand the wisdom behind it that they are trying to share with you and utilize that wisdom in your favor.

When everyone was telling us to stop and consider the consequences of leaving our careers and our stability to take that first trip around the world, I took it as, "What happens if you come back and find yourself broke and jobless?" That fear was most definitely not going to stop my hubby or me from living out our dreams, however, it would have been foolish not to have a back-up plan. So, we saved. We saved for the trip and for our return. We planned on 10 months with no income, a few for the trip, and the rest for when we return. We didn't burn any bridges with employers or clients and most certainly we didn't act irresponsibly. Why? First of all, never burn bridges. Second of all, you never know when you can help someone or when someone can help you. We took the advice given and applied it to our own situation. Not that we hadn't thought of it ourselves, but just to reaffirm our own ideas. These savings gave us the inner safety to spend freely on our trip and to know that we had a backup while we picked up our careers again upon returning.

Both of these examples are financial, since that is one of the major fears people have, but the idea applies to everything you are trying to do. Sometimes, you just need to break free from everything holding you back and jump headlong into your dreams. That is OK, too! Just remember to listen and trust your instincts. If somethings feels wrong, it may be because it is.

Remember that your parents and loved ones' ideas of success don't have to match yours. We live in a different world from when they were our age. We are also completely different people with different circumstances. It's only natural that our dreams are different from theirs. Listen to your heart and don't let anyone else impose his or her dreams on you. As the amazing grown up and #smartgirl that you are, make sure you are not letting your ego dictate your way rather than your heart. You know better.

Now that you've taken that guilt out of the picture, fully accepted yourself for who you are and what your dreams are, let's dive deeper into how to deal with your family when their idea for your life doesn't match yours.

Setting Boundaries

Let's face it, sometimes you can't just cut off communication with your family to have the breathing space you need to grow. In my case, I know my mom would be at my door knocking if I stopped answering the phone for a week.

So, what other option do you have?

Setting ground rules that will give you the space you need to become who you need to be without their constant disapproval bringing you down.

The first step you can take is talking to them. Ask your mom (or dad, or whomever is not on board with your plans) to a coffee (or wine) date and share your dreams and aspirations. Help your family understand that you are covering all your bases with a plan B and C just in case, but that your plan A is what makes the world go around for you. Open up your heart.

Express your why, your how, and as much as you know at the moment. Share everything you've learned about yourself and the world in the past few weeks. Share your new views of the world. Share with them where you are placing your values now and what that brings to the table for you. Share how much happier you are since you accepted who you are and how you want that to move forward for you. Share this book with them if you think it might help. Sometimes complete transparency can be counter-intuitive, but it can also be the best option!

Remember to bring tissues! This might become a turning point in your life and in your relationship with your family. They might be more supportive than you think! I have realized that they mainly don't want to see you suffer and fail. Presenting them the plan you are following will make them see you as an adult who has reached a certain level of maturity and now is making adult decisions, not just a kid running around following every impulse.

What if they are not receptive to your ideas and still don't back you up? Maybe you don't have the kind of relationship with them just to sit down and pour your heart open. I still advise you to try it since it may be the key to unlocking that trust between the two of you. Even if that is not the case, not all is lost.

Instead of pouring your soul out to them, or if doing it didn't get them on board, have them agree not to touch "sensitive" subjects. For example, if they are calling you, have them not ask you how your diet is going (if you are removing that vocabulary from your life) or have them not ask you career questions if they won't like the answer, etc. The same goes for all aspects of your life that you are trying to change and that they don't agree with.

It might feel sometimes that there is a big elephant in the room, however, it is only awkward if you allow it! There are plenty of other subjects you can talk about. This helps not leaving everyone involved with heartache at the end. Talk about happy things and things that bring you joy and bring you closer together. Ask for recipes and ask how everyone is doing. Let them know about the last movie you watched or your plans for the weekend. Maybe share your cousin's engagement announcement and ask about your grandma's health. Whatever you do, make sure you both know that certain topics won't be discussed for the good of all involved; your intention is to bring you guys closer, not to fight every time.

If while on a family visit, or on any given day, they do mention those "forbidden" topics and insist on giving you advice about how you are doing things wrong, remember they are doing it out of love. Simply smile and nod. You've done your due diligence by letting them know in advance. They have just proven they are not willing to change. Don't waste your precious energy arguing yet again. Simply smile, nod, and retire, even if it hurts. Remember that you are not doing anything wrong. Allow whatever feeling comes to the surface to exist for under a minute. Let it dissolve and recite your why. I promise this eventually will become automatic for you until you reach a point where no negative feelings come at all ;) I pinky promise! While negative feelings still come, turn to your tribe! Tag your tribe with #rebellifestyledesign and you'll have our full support to get your through whatever it is you're going through! You are not alone!

If all else fails, call less often or ask them for some time off. Tell them you'll be crazy busy on a project for a month and that you'll report daily with a text that you are alive, but they shouldn't call for a while.

If you haven't already, move out. You need to give yourself the space you need to become who you truly are in every aspect. This is done not by following others' rules in their home, but by establishing your own. This gives you an unparalleled insight into who you truly are, from the way you decorate your new place to what rules you set in place. You will have the freedom to be yourself fully, while at the same time learning to appreciate your parents more when you do spend some time together.

On another note, I'm sorry to break it to you, Girl, but another minute you spend in their house, another minute you are becoming more like your mom or dad. Not only in a good way, but also in the little things that annoyed you while growing up and still push your buttons to this day. Honey, you are doing them now and you know it. Get your own place and develop your own annoying habits your kids will hate. Give yourself the gift of space to become who you were truly meant to be.

You Love Them

One of my mom's biggest dreams has been to go to Paris. For as long as I can remember, she has talked about seeing the Eiffel Tower and strolling through the streets in the iconic city. My dad, on the other hand, is not too fond of flying. Even though they have been on vacations, this has resulted in my mom's dream staying only a dream.

Two years ago, I stood right where she's always wanted to go. I was sitting across from the Eiffel Tower with a glass of wine in one hand and the tastiest cheese in the other. Baguettes and sweets were laid down on our picnic mat. I knew at that moment that I needed to help my mom make it there.

Ever since I returned, I have been talking to my mom about how she needs to go for her dreams and just go to Paris. She sees my insistence not as those from a naïve kid just saying, "Mom, why don't you just do it?" It's coming from an experienced traveler who has made it there saying, "Mom, why don't you just do it?" She now believes it's possible because I've done it.

At first, I wanted to take her. I thought she could just come with us on a second trip to Paris, but she wants to go with my dad as well. They are a #relationshipgoals couple after all. I kept insisting she go, and she kept coming up with reasons not to. Her latest reason for saying no has been that she now wants us all to go together as a family, the seven of us counting plus ones. So far, it has been simply conversation, but every time we talk about it, I find her more and more willing.

This year my parents celebrated their 35th anniversary. Mom called me a few months prior to tell me about how she wanted to get married again, to my dad obviously, and have a huge wedding. She was going to have this incredible party at an amazing venue, do all the planning again, the flowers, the church, the invitations, the three-course meal, open bar, invite everyone she knew, the whole deal and wanted me to help her. My first reaction was, "How much are you spending??" After she answered, and I got over the initial shock of spending so much money feeding all those people (sorry I-have-dreamed-about-my-wedding-since-I-was-5 girls—I'm not one of you), I said, "Mom, why don't you use that money and we ALL go to Paris like you've always dreamed of?"

Her voice changed. There was shock, excitement, and hesitation all at the same time. There was a tiny ray of hope like when you feel like you screwed up an interview until one of your friends shares with you her worst interview and suddenly you believe you could get a call back... "I'll talk to your dad! You'd plan the whole thing, right? I mean, you've been there. You have to tell us where to go. Yes, let's do it. I want to go to Rome, too. OK, let me talk to your dad!"

THE ONLY REASON MY MOM BELIEVED HER DREAM WAS MORE THAN JUST OPTIMISTIC IDEAS OF A LIFE SHE'D NEVER HAVE WAS BECAUSE I HAD SHARED MY DREAMS WITH HER AND THEN WENT ON TO ACHIEVE THEM. THAT GAVE HER PERMISSION TO BELIEVE HER DREAMS COULD BECOME A REALITY, TOO.

This October, the whole family is taking our first family trip involving a plane in over five years—since my wedding in Cancun. We are going to France and Italy for a couple of weeks to make my mom's dream a reality.

The only reason my mom believed her dream was more than just optimistic ideas of a life she'd never have was because I had shared my dreams with her and then went on to achieve them. That gave her permission to believe her dreams could become a reality, too.

On our last phone conversation, I was sharing with my mom all of my new plans for a new business idea, leaving the country again, and a lot of other crazy stuff that goes through my head, and she said "Well honey, you've always accomplished everything you've ever set your eyes on. This won't be any different."

Even after completely rebelling against her during my teenage years (seriously—poor woman) and again in my adult life by doing the opposite of most of her teachings and still refusing to produce a grandchild, she is proud of the woman I've become.

She still sometimes wishes I were more like her idea of me, but that's just who she is. We've both learned that. Most importantly, we don't let it affect our relationship anymore. We are actually closer than ever.

Having a family is an amazing blessing that we sometimes take for granted. You love them. That is why it hurts sometimes when they don't back you up in your most important dreams and aspirations. You want them to feel proud of you and you want to make them happy at the same time. Just remember that you can't pour from an empty cup. You need to work on yourself first. Accomplish your dreams and goals, love yourself to death, and become the best person you can possibly be. Then, help them do the same. You are doing it as much for them as for you.

PARIS

PARIS

CHAPTER 13

Roadblock #5 – You

You've probably seen this coming since the start. You are the smartest girl on the planet and you already figured out after reading all of the previous chapters that the common denominator in all of your fears, and all of the ways these fears present themselves, is YOU.

You hold the keys to your own happiness. You alone have the power to change the narrative in your head, turn fear around, and make it your bitch instead of your handler.

Our minds are like hyperactive kids on cocaine—not ever stopping the constant thoughts and chatter. Some of it is useful. A lot of it is bullshit. A lot of it is recreating scenarios, imagining scenarios about fights that didn't happen, saying the things we should have said, or regretting the words we did say. A lot of it is planning

YOU HOLD THE KEYS TO YOUR OWN HAPPINESS. YOU ALONE HAVE THE POWER TO CHANGE THE NARRATIVE IN YOUR HEAD, TURN FEAR AROUND, AND MAKE IT YOUR BITCH INSTEAD OF YOUR HANDLER.

for the future. THE MAJORITY OF IT is judging ourselves. This is why we become our biggest roadblocks. We let those wild, drug-induced-child-minds run free and allow ourselves to believe everything that comes out of them.

We constantly sabotage ourselves on our own path to fulfillment and we don't even realize it. You can come up with reasons like lack of money, time, support, your partner, and whatever else you can think of, instead of realizing that the only thing standing between you and your dreams is yourself.

I established only one rule at the beginning of the book: this is a judgment-free zone. You are not to judge anyone else. Especially, you are not to judge yourself. I know you know, but this seemed like a good time to remind you.

Get Out of Your Own Way

Let me get super real with you. I'm not writing this book so you can read it, find some of the ideas interesting, and then move on with your life as it has been until now. I'm writing this book because I seriously want you to get off your ass and work toward your dreams, F-ing what everyone says about them, and start living your most authentic life.

Why? Because I know it's possible. Because I've done it. Because you are meant for so much more in your life and I don't want you to look back at 45 and feel like you wasted the last 20 years. Hell, I don't want you to pick this book up again in a year and realize all of the progress you could have made already if you'd only followed your plan. I've been there and it SUCKS. Let's not allow that asshole of your mind to play tricks on you and tear down your commitment to your dreams.

I believe in the power of timing. I believe I'm writing this book at the right time for me and I believe you are reading it at the perfect time for you. This is your time to make your dreams a reality. Now. You made it this far. You are already winning!!

You have set yourself up for success by coming up with a plan to accomplish your goals—down to the daily tasks. You love yourself in ways you never thought possible. You have figured out how to carve out more money and time to get things done.

You have created a tribe online and offline. Even family is either at kept at bay or right there as the cheerleading squad. You are on your way to the life of your dreams where you can be the truest you possible.

You start, full of excitement, just like that girl with her shoe store a few chapters ago. You are committed to making her ending not be yours. You got this! In order for you not to end up like her, let's take a hard look at what really happened to her.

The simple answer is that she let her own head get in the way and ended up believing every single negative thought she had, plus the ones everyone around her had, until eventually she convinced herself that her dream wasn't worth pursuing any longer. She wasn't worth it any longer. That won't be you because by now you know better.

The day will come, however, when the challenges feel far greater than the progress or when you get your first, or 34th, "NO," when even with your full-on tribe supporting you, and everything around you telling you it's possible, your mind will play into your fears and it will tell you that it just may not be possible for you—that you are not good enough.

It will do this through negative thoughts and self-judgment, through self-sabotage and procrastination, through paralyzing overwhelm. These are all playing into your fears. Fear of failure, fear of success, fear of the unknown. If you are not prepared for it, they will tear you down because that is what fear does.

You have identified your biggest fears through the exercise in Chapter 8 and know by now that a lot of it is in YOUR HEAD. *That back-stabbing bitch.* Our minds can sabotage our dreams on a daily basis—just like for shoe girl.

Let's go over how to switch every fear-inducing thought or action that presents itself as sabotage and turn it around to help us achieve our goals.

Limiting Beliefs

A limiting belief is when you tell yourself that it is "not possible" for you to do something, when in fact, it is possible. For example:

"I won't ever be a millionaire."

"I can't just drop everything and leave."

"I can't just dye my hair pink."

"I won't ever find another guy to love me like he does."

"I can't change careers now."

"That won't ever work."

"That's a guy's job."

"I can't do this."

"People don't love their jobs."

"I have to be skinny to be happy."

"I will never visit Mykonos."

"I can't."

...and many more.

This is one of the most common ways I hear that fear stops people from acting. A lot of times I'm talking to people about our travels, telling them exactly how we did it, the exact methods we use to plan, about points, miles, and savings and the first thing out of their mouths with eyes of disbelief is, "Wow, that is awesome! I would LOVE to go to Mykonos, but I could never do that."

Then comes a supposed valid reason to reinforce the limiting belief:

"I have a good job right now. I can't just leave."

"I don't have a job right now. I can't afford it."

"I don't have anyone to go with me."

"Hubby hates to travel."

"I have other stuff going on right now."

"I could never save that kind of money."

"That is not for people like me."

I get it. Traveling is not everyone's dream like it is for me. Not everyone will make it a priority. When the people who do dream about traveling and visiting the Greek islands, as well as everywhere else we have been, say that to me, my heart aches a little for them.

I'm not saying that all of the above are not true, however, it is true for most of us. I had a job and Yahir didn't love traveling (hard to believe now, right?). I had clients and projects going on and didn't know the first thing about saving. So why was I able to accomplish my traveling goals? Now people look at me like I did something incredible like flying to the moon!

All I did was do a lot of research. I took out a bunch of credit cards with hefty sign up bonuses and made sure to book first class tickets with those bonuses (which was completely optional). I saved a part of our income, convinced Yahir, my boss, and my clients that we would return to continue life as usual after a couple of months. That was it. Seriously, anyone can do that. (If I'm completely honest, the hardest part was Yahir.)

Do you know what I did before all that? The one thing that was absolutely crucial to everything that came after?

I BELIEVED it was possible.

DO YOU KNOW WHAT I DID BEFORE ALL THAT? THE ONE THING THAT WAS ABSOLUTELY CRUCIAL TO EVERYTHING THAT CAME AFTER?

I BELIEVED IT WAS POSSIBLE.

BECAUSE I BELIEVED IT WAS POSSIBLE, I FOUND A WAY TO MAKE IT HAPPEN.

Because I believed it was possible, I found a way to make it happen. That is true for a lot of things in my life, like doing it again by writing this book.

I didn't let any limiting belief come into my head and mess up my crazy dreams to travel the world in style and leave everything behind. On the contrary, to every single negative comment and every single mini second of doubt, I said "but... what if I can?" Then, I went on to find ways to make it happen.

That is how you turn your limiting beliefs around and use them to fuel your dreams. Just by second guessing them!! Second guessing is like second nature for a lot of us!

Every lonely night when your mind is trying to play tricks on you and you start getting doubts about what you are doing, simply ask yourself, "What if I CAN?" "What if I AM worthy?" "What if I MAKE it?" Once you have planted the seed of possibility, and you are on your way back to the light, go further and believe it.

Start by looking at your social media account where you only follow inspirational people and brands. If you haven't done this yet, start one now! Use those accounts as your vision board. Have them show you how possible it is to live the life you imagine! Focus on the things that you may have in common with them. Look up their bios. There must be someone who was where you are right now who broke through it to accomplish all of

EVERY LONELY NIGHT WHEN YOUR MIND IS TRYING TO PLAY TRICKS ON YOU AND YOU START GETTING DOUBTS ABOUT WHAT YOU ARE DOING, SIMPLY ASK YOURSELF, "WHAT IF I CAN?" "WHAT IF I AM WORTHY?" "WHAT IF I MAKE IT?" ONCE YOU HAVE PLANTED THE SEED OF POSSIBILITY, AND YOU ARE ON YOUR WAY BACK TO THE LIGHT, GO FURTHER AND BELIEVE IT.

his or her goals. Send that person a private message and say how much you appreciate what he or she does. Ask the person something. You just might get an answer.

Read a book about overcoming limiting beliefs! Watch a movie about a book that talks about this. I watched the movie "The Secret" about 10 years ago and can confidently say that it was one of those moments that changed the way I look at the world. To this day, I practice all of the daily activities suggested in the movie and can confidently say that your mind has the power to create anything you want in this life—not out of magic, but through believing extraordinary things are possible. You begin to find new ways to achieve what you want.

One of the most powerful practices I first learned in that movie, and have read in countless other books about achieving goals, was visualization. By visualizing yourself doing the things you want to be doing, even the tough ones, having the things you want to have, and letting your imagination fill in the gaps, you actively turn that vision into a reality. I do this every morning. I visualize my day going smoothly and see myself powering through my to-do list. Try it!

Don't ever stop practicing exercise #1! Reaffirm to yourself that you are worthy of your dreams! Remember that if you do it in front of the mirror, while naked, you give yourself extra power!!

Even if you don't believe it at that moment, say to yourself, "Today, you may not be sure of what you can accomplish. Know that you can do anything you set your mind to because you are worthy of your dreams."

Recite your why E-V-E-R-Y D-A-Y!! This is a limiting belief kryptonite! ;)

Lastly, remember your tribe! Share your struggles with them. Share with them online or offline and have them help you get through them. They are there for you! You can also share with our community and we'll be there to help you power through whatever you are going through! You've got this, Girl! ☺

Procrastination

One of the most common ways we tend to sabotage ourselves, in absolutely everything we do, is through procrastination. I should know—I'm a master procrastinator. I built a whole business idea around it. The root of this procrastination, just like everything else we've been talking about in these last few chapters, is fear.

In this case, fear acts so subtly, yet powerfully, making us believe that the important stuff doesn't need to get done *right now*. This makes it far easier for us to binge watch all seasons of "How I Met Your Mother" (yet again) instead of sitting down and doing your task of the day. I have spent hours upon hours Googling "important stuff" and "researching" instead of sitting down and actually getting stuff done. Why? Because the stuff that I needed to get done was so important, like writing this book, that procrastination became a daily struggle in my life. I convinced myself that I was busy when I was just wasting time.

I was finally doing something that was so deep and powerful and so out of my comfort zone that my subconscious did the best it could to stop me by projecting fear into my days through procrastination.

The problem is not that you take a day longer to achieve your goals. The real problem is that when you have a bad day, work was much more stressful than usual, you got into a fight with the significant other, your girlfriend got a pregnancy scare, your mom asks about your love life even though it's in the "forbidden categories," or you are totally hungover from drinks last night... then you decide to take a day off your dream life plans.

You let that bad day change your plans and get into your sacred time of "dream life tasks." Since the first one is always the hardest, next time something bad happens you change your plans yet again. All of a sudden, you've let that one bad day turn into two, then three, then you figure it's Wednesday. "I'll start again next Monday," and throw the whole week. That week turns into a month. Before you know it, it's been six months since the last time you recited your WHY and gave yourself some mirror self-love.

Unfortunately, we let ourselves forget that we only live one life.

There is a limited number of years in our existence. Each should be treated as sacred because no moment is ever coming back.

I once heard a story about a 45-year-old woman who had been with her husband for 25 years yet was deeply unhappy in her relationship. They fought all the time making the whole atmosphere in the house toxic for them and not the best example for their kid. Instead of changing her circumstances though, she decided she was not going to get a divorce; she had chosen him as her partner and she was staying put, continuing life as usual. That wouldn't stop her from complaining every day at work about her unhappy marriage.

UNFORTUNATELY, WE LET OURSELVES FORGET THAT WE ONLY LIVE ONE LIFE.

THERE IS A LIMITED NUMBER OF YEARS IN OUR EXISTENCE. EACH SHOULD BE TREATED AS SACRED BECAUSE NO MOMENT IS EVER COMING BACK.

THAT IS WHAT PROCRASTINATION DOES—IT KEEPS YOU COZY IN YOUR COMFORT ZONE, EVEN IF YOU ARE UNHAPPY IN IT, WHILE ALLOWING TIME TO JUST SLIP BY WHILE NOTHING CHANGES AROUND YOU.

Now, there is nothing wrong with fighting for the love of your life, or for your dream life, but only if you are in fact fighting. I mean, if you are only complaining about your life and doing absolutely nothing to change it, then you are allowing time to go by while you sit there and watch it happen.

That is what procrastination does—it keeps you cozy in your comfort zone, even if you are unhappy in it, while allowing time to just slip by while nothing changes around you. and most certainly while those dreams never actually materialize.

The best way to avoid procrastination is by holding ourselves accountable. Either through an accountability partner or on our own by putting in place the right methods. Be completely honest with yourself about which one of the two you need. For me, it is external accountability. I have a couple of accountability partners. I know some people who are disciplined enough to do it on their own.

The first thing you need to do to conquer procrastination is have a clear action plan for every day. That is why we focused on that in the workbook. If you haven't done those exercises, please go to momisnotalwaysright.com/resources and get them done asap. They are super important!

Once you know what you are supposed to do each day, establish specific time-blocks in your day to tackle your daily activities. By knowing the exact time you'll do each activity daily, you'll be able to treat this time as "do not touch" and give your goal your full attention. Also, specify exactly where you'll do this work. According to Marie Forleo, knowing where you'll do the work increases your chances of being successful.

Create a one-month calendar, or download our cool version at momisnotalwaysright.com/resources, and put it up by your bed. Write your top three activities per day. Put a check on the ones you managed to do and a big X on the day when you do all three. If you get 5 Xes in a row, celebrate!! Get a massage. Take yourself out for dinner. Chill for a day knowing your dreams are coming true! ☺

If you become your own accountability buddy, set time each Sunday to review the week. Make notes about what worked well and what didn't work well during the week. If some days you were not able to follow through with the plan, instead of giving yourself a hard time, simply re-adjust as needed and keep going!

Another tip: set reminders on your phone at different times each day reminding you of how awesome you are, your why, and what you need to get done for the day. This will lighten up your day and keep you focused on your dreams. It's an awesome little reminder ;)

If you have an external accountability partner, make sure your partner knows what you are supposed to be doing each day and when so your partner can hold you accountable. Share your goals, your why, and the tasks at hand. Your partner also is there for you when those limiting beliefs come crawling in.

This accountability partner can be a friend, lover, cousin, or a community of accountability partners. Accountability makes you feel a sense of urgency to make you act on your goals instead of postponing them—much like when you did your homework in school only because the teacher was going to check. If you need help finding an accountability partner, tag us on the community and will do our best to get you matched up! ;) #accountabilitypartner

Lastly, remember that procrastination is a symptom of an underlying fear. It is within your power not to let it control you. Procrastination is not the real enemy, but it can become a true burden if you let it. Set yourself up for success by putting in place the systems that will make you achieve your goals.

Fear of the Unknown

When I was a small girl, I was 100%, hardcore afraid of the dark. I couldn't bear the thought of going to bed in pitch darkness! It would drive me crazy that all the lights were turned off! It scared the shit out of me! It wasn't the darkness itself that scared me, it was not knowing what was hiding in the darkness.

My imagination went to all the places it could think of from crazy clowns to ghosts, to killers, to the boogeyman, to whomever-was-the-bad-guy in the last horror movie I'd seen. I wouldn't move a finger because I thought that if there were something hiding in the darkness, I would prefer not to let it know I was awake. I would lay there, paralyzed by fear, not being able to fall asleep or do anything else.

Some nights, when I couldn't take it any longer, I would gather all my courage and make it from my bed to the door to turn the light on. Everything was all right with the world again!! Seeing that there was nothing scary in my bedroom, I could go to bed. While still a bit afraid, I could easily fall asleep in minutes! Those nights that I didn't make it out of bed to turn on the lights, however, were long and horrific!

Imagination is one of the most powerful tools of fear. Imagination can fuel fear and makes that fear become so real in our bodies that you can almost touch it! Imagination, and these imaginary scenes of pain and death, are very real as adults as well. You may not be afraid of the dark anymore, but fear is still tangible in different things and for different reasons.

Fear of failure, fear of success, fear of making a fool of yourself... all these fears have in common that we don't really know what is going to happen. Our imagination comes up with the worst possible scenario. Just like a little girl hiding in her bed, it paralyzes you and keeps you from acting.

Just like turning the light on was the solution to my fear, because I now could see clearly what was there and what wasn't, fear of the unknown also is kept in check through clarity.

We get overwhelmed with doubts, questions, what ifs, and all sorts of other thinking. We can't seem to move forward because there is no clear path from the bottom of the staircase to the top where our dream life lies.

Let me tell you, every single day of your existence is your dream life simply because you exist and are here to enjoy it. You are making your decisions based on your heart and what you truly want. Because you've already done the 30-day challenge, for at least the last 30 days, you have been making massive progress in your life. Remember that.

THE IMPORTANT THING WE FORGET WHEN WE GET OVERWHELMED IS THAT EVERYTHING GETS ACCOMPLISHED BY TAKING ONE STEP AT A TIME. FORGET ABOUT THE TOP OF THE STAIRS AND FOCUS ON TAKING THAT FIRST STEP. ONCE YOU TAKE THE FIRST, TAKE THE NEXT, AND THEN THE NEXT, AND THE NEXT ALL THE WAY TO THE TOP. ONE AT A TIME.

As far as reaching the bigger goals you have set for yourself, the important thing we forget when we get overwhelmed is that everything gets accomplished by taking one step at a time.

Forget about the top of the stairs and focus on taking that first step. Once you take the first, take the next, and then the next, and the next all the way to the top. One at a time. Focus your energy on your daily activities that you have planned; you'll see how it will all unfold by itself.

The easiest and fastest way to obtain clarity—that works just as fast as turning on the light in a dark room—is asking. When you are feeling like the world will end unless you do what you are supposed to but have no idea what to do next, remember that you are not alone. There is someone out there who has been in your shoes. Ask for advice!

Reach out to your tribe. It's OK to be vulnerable with the right people. Open up with those who will push you forward and bounce ideas off of each other. This can be a close friend, your significant other, your accountability partner, or anyone else in the online world.

Check out some of the people you follow. Maybe they have blogs where they talk about how they got from where you are to where they are now. Maybe a podcast or a YouTube channel. Reach to their communities or ask them directly for advice. Never hesitate to reach out! Ask for advice from someone who has accomplished it and you might be surprised at how much clarity you get!

You also can hire a coach. The whole reason coaches exist, at least the good ones, is to enlighten people on their path to goal accomplishment by offering accountability, clarity, a winning game plan, and tackling mindset barriers. They are where you want to go and are there to show you the way. If you find it within your means, hire a coach to help you get there in a less painful and a faster way. The truth is, if the coach is good, you'll end up saving the coaching fee many times over with the time the coach saves you and the money decisions the coach will help you make.

Remember that we also are here for you! We are your community as well. Tag us in your post using #rebellifestyledesign and let us know your troubles and what's keeping you up at night. Our community is always delighted to help and solve doubts. I also would love to help you if possible. No one was born knowing all the answers.

One very important thing to keep in mind is that you are going to learn more and more as you follow your path. It is perfectly OK to adjust the plans along the way! You don't need to know every single detail from the start. Some things build off of each other; that is fine.

As you take more steps and start to get clarity on the things you didn't know, adjust the plan accordingly and keep going.

Simply don't give up! More importantly, don't let the lack of knowledge stop you from taking those first steps sending you into "analysis paralysis" (re-read the "Procrastination" section in this chapter).

When I get overwhelmed, I journal. I hash out all of my feelings on paper and get clear on what it is that is causing fear in me. Once I allow my thoughts to come and go and give room for my feelings to exist instead of fighting them in my head, I realize that most of the time, it is the bigger task that feels like it's just going to be too much or like it's impossible to accomplish. That is when I need a break.

The last time that happened, I went shopping with a friend. We met at the mall because she needed help picking out changing tables for her new baby. She's a first-time mom and I'm completely oblivious to motherhood. We failed miserably, but we had so much fun! We had some laughs, talked life, and by completely focusing on her and what she needed, I was able to get out of my head and relax. Giving is incredible!

I suggest that when you are feeling overwhelmed, and you already tried talking it out with yourself through journaling or meditating or with someone else like your partner, a friend, or your accountability buddy, a break is efficient and important!

YOU ARE ABLE TO ACCOMPLISH
EVERYTHING YOU WANT IN
YOUR LIFE. EVEN WITH FEARS,
HESITATION, OVERWHELM, AND
THE WHOLE WORLD AGAINST YOU.
YOU ARE WHAT YOU BELIEVE YOU
ARE. MAKE SURE YOU BELIEVE
THAT YOU ARE WORTHY, THAT YOU
ARE BEAUTIFUL, THAT YOU CAN
DO ANYTHING, AND THAT YOU ARE
GOING TO LIVE YOUR BEST LIFE
STARTING NOW, BECAUSE YOU CAN.

Take a break. Go out with your friends. Have lunch with your significant other. Visit an old friend. Hit the gym. Talk to other people about themselves. Do something that brings joy to your life and gets you out of your head. By focusing on others, you are not only giving them the attention they deserve, you are also helping yourself get relaxed and back on track. ;)

You've Got This

You are able to accomplish everything you want in your life. Even with fears, hesitation, overwhelm, and the whole world against you. You are what you believe you are. Make sure you believe that you are worthy, that you are beautiful, that you can do anything, and that you are going to live your best life starting now, because YOU CAN.

Even when those fears come, remember. Remember your worth. Remember you are not alone. We all experience negative thoughts. We all have fears. The difference between those who make it and those who don't is knowing when to pay attention to the thoughts and when to dismiss them because they are not serving you. Self-love and self-care are the first steps to your dream life. It all starts with believing your worth.

Lastly, CELEBRATE! Whenever you achieve a small or a big milestone, celebrate! Celebrate life and celebrate your uniqueness. Celebrate your triumph over fear time and time again, even when you feel you didn't triumph. The mere act of realizing it puts you one step ahead. Celebrate and share with your tribe! Girl, you've got this!

As a side note, and in the effort of helping you if you are feeling overwhelmed, I want to share something real with you. I wish I could say that I've outgrown my fear of the dark. I haven't. I seriously haven't.

If I'm being completely transparent with you, I'm a big scary baby in grown-up clothes. I still turn all the lights on if I'm by myself so there are no dark rooms. I also turn on the TV or some music really loud to fill up the space with noise. That's OK for me.

From one girl full of "silly" fears to another, know that your fears do not make you any less worthy, or capable, of achieving of your dreams.

FROM ONE GIRL FULL OF "SILLY" FEARS TO ANOTHER, KNOW THAT YOUR FEARS DO NOT MAKE YOU ANY LESS WORTHY, OR CAPABLE, OF ACHIEVING OF YOUR DREAMS.

MYKONOS

MYKONOS

CHAPTER 14

What Is The Worst That Could Happen?

Think about the dream that you are working on. Seriously, just think of it. Think about it becoming a reality. Think about how good that will be, how awesome it will feel, and how life-changing it is going to be.

Now, think about the worst thing that could happen if it failed. Did you die? Did you wreck your life in unfixable ways? If it is not this bad, then you are probably OK.

This is a little experiment that Yahir and I do every time we are about to do something crazy and out of the ordinary. We sit down, and in a thinking-out-loud kind of way, ask "What is the worst that could happen?"

For example:

What is the worst that could happen if we moved to Malaysia for one month followed by one month in Budapest trying our luck as digital nomads?

1. We may fail miserably.
2. We may run out of our savings if those projects don't come through while we are away. Then, we would be forced to come back to the states early only to realize that clients didn't wait for us and be forced to find 9 – 5s while maxing out our credit cards to live.
3. We may hate it there. We may hate the food, the people, and the countries themselves. We may completely regret our decision and be miserable for the whole stay.

Seriously... that is not so bad.

I know of people who live like this every day and so do you: projects don't come through, they don't have any savings, live off of their maxed-out credit cards, and are miserable in their day-to-day lives.

If the worst-case scenario of following a crazy dream is to end up living like the large majority of us already do, then quite honestly, I'm jumping on that train, fast—because it's worth it, because the worst-case scenario doesn't involve dying or hurting anyone.

The only thing I have to lose is some time and money. Things that we end up wasting, even if we are safely at home, by spending mindless hours watching Netflix or buying things we really don't need to impress people we don't really like.

WHAT IS THE WORST THAT COULD HAPPEN IF YOU DECIDED TO FOLLOW YOUR DREAMS?

On the other hand, it just might work. It just might be an awesome outcome and I'll be glad I did it after all. Even if it fails, that adventure of chasing a dream will be incredible and I'll learn so much!

Do the exercise yourself. What is the worst that could happen if you decided to follow your dreams?

Maybe you cut ties with some important people and the worst that could happen is that you get banned from certain social circles. Were they really that important? Were they draining your energy instead of supporting you? Maybe this worst-case scenario is a good thing, rather than a nightmare.

Maybe it's really bad because you alienated your family or your coworkers now think you are a stuck-up bitch from not wanting to get happy hour drinks with them. Is the situation unmanageable? Can you just start going again? Maybe you realize you are happier avoiding that social interaction entirely.

What if you quit your job and all of a sudden your dreams fail miserably? Would your savings account go into red numbers? Would you have to move back home? Can you handle that?

What if you move across the world to follow your passion, and once you get there, you realize it is not at all what you thought. Would you be devasted? Would there be no one you can count on? Can you just get on a plane and go back home?

This is about taking full responsibility for your life and everything in it. It's about very adult-ly taking a look at your plans and asking yourself, "What is the worst that could happen if I decide to follow my dreams?"

If that outcome is manageable for you—if you can live with it— then there is no real risk. There is only upwards from there. You go back to your old job, or get a new one. You charge a couple of months on that credit card. You get new friends because you stopped talking to your old ones. Your family interactions are a little weird now because you told some truths, but they'll get over it eventually. You made a fool of yourself socially by announcing your dreams to the world and now that they've failed it hurts when people keep asking about them with, "I told you so" eyes. You love yourself so much now that, just for a second, it all seems worth it.

The truth is, we let ourselves feel so vulnerable and scared with the unknown that we become our own worst roadblock. In reality, the worst-case scenario may not be that scary at all.

THE TRUTH IS, WE LET OURSELVES FEEL SO VULNERABLE AND SCARED WITH THE UNKNOWN THAT WE BECOME OUR OWN WORST ROADBLOCK. IN REALITY, THE WORST-CASE SCENARIO MAY NOT BE THAT SCARY AT ALL.

It may be real. It may have serious consequences. The truth is, quite probably you won't die. You will have grown and you will have learned. You will come out the other side a little bruised and a little beaten, but you'll be better for it. If you decide, after analyzing your own worst-case scenario, that you can live with it, is there a risk?

I seriously advise that you spend a good 30 minutes stating your worst-case scenario. Mind map it, journal it, or simply say it out loud. Face that fear right in the eyes and decide right then if you can live with it. If so, jump on that train.

BUDAPEST

MALAYSIA

CHAPTER 15

What Is The Best That Could Happen?

Now, let's flip the script. After spending some time analyzing your worst-case scenario, take a look at the other end of the spectrum. What is the best that could happen if you in fact decided to woman-up and follow your dreams?

Are you the person you wish you were?

Are you living where you want to be living?

Is your work now fundamentally more soul-enriching?

Are your relationships better?

Are you happy and fulfilled?

WHAT IS THE BEST THAT COULD HAPPEN IF YOU IN FACT DECIDED TO WOMAN-UP AND FOLLOW YOUR DREAMS?

Give yourself permission to dream and to imagine the good things.

The best that could happen is that you find yourself living a life you love, on your own terms, surrounded by your real tribe.

You found great new friends who help you and teach you to be better each day. You surrounded yourself with amazing people who lift you up. You do the same for them. You are now so happy to post and share your wins and challenges because your tribe is always there for you.

You love your work and it fills you with joy. You don't hate Mondays anymore. On the contrary, you love what you do and the days of the week mean nothing when you are doing something you are truly passionate about.

You live where you've always dreamed of and your environment makes you smile every single morning. You have to pinch yourself at times to believe that this is in fact your life because it is so awesome.

IT'S TIME, GIRL.

IT'S TIME YOU LET GO OF YOUR OLD WAYS.

IT'S TIME YOU LET GO OF SELF-JUDGMENT.

IT'S TIME YOU LET GO OF OTHERS' JUDGMENT.

IT'S TIME YOU LET GO OF NEGATIVE SELF-TALK.

IT'S TIME YOU LET GO OF TOXIC PEOPLE.

IT'S TIME YOU LET GO OF THE WHAT IFS.

IT'S TIME YOU LET GO OF IMPOSED EXPECTATIONS.

IT'S TIME YOU LET GO OF THE THOUGHT THAT YOU CAN
CONTROL WHAT EVERYONE AROUND YOU THINKS.

IT'S TIME YOU LET GO OF LIVING THE LIFE YOU'VE BEEN
LIVING UP UNTIL THIS MOMENT IF THAT LIFE ISN'T
FILLED WITH LOVE AND POSITIVITY.

IT'S TIME TO LET GO OF THE PAST.

You wake up so full of confidence and self-love that every decision you make day after day, from what to wear to what to eat, is easy since the answer is always "What is best for me?" You feel and act as the most beautiful girl on earth, because you know you are!

You have an amazing exercise routine that you do out of love for yourself. You never go to the gym to "punish" your body from eating that treat the day before, but rather you move your body to help it heal and thrive. You do everything out of love and appreciation for your body and for the work it does for you.

You have an incredible guilt-free relationship with your mom. Your continuous heart to heart talks with her have taught you both that you are different people, but the love for each other is so great that you are now closer than ever. Even though you still don't do what she says, she supports you in your endeavors and you feel happy every time you go home.

You have a partner who fully supports you. You no longer accept sleeping with assholes who don't respect you. After loving yourself so much, you've learned to accept only mutual respect and love from your partner. You have found someone who truly loves you for who you are. You are an incredible team helping each other achieve your goals.

Every morning, you stand naked in front of the mirror and you tell yourself how beautiful you are, how much you love yourself, and why you are doing the things you are doing in your life. You don't have to convince yourself of the words; they are carved in your heart and you feel them as your own unique reality. You are filled with so much love and peace that you project that in everything that you do.

Isn't it worth it?

It's Time to Let Go

It's time, Girl.

It's time you let go of your old ways.

It's time you let go of self-judgment.

It's time you let go of others' judgment.

It's time you let go of negative self-talk.

It's time you let go of toxic people.

It's time you let go of the what ifs.

It's time you let go of imposed expectations.

It's time you let go of the thought that you can control what everyone around you thinks.

It's time you let go of living the life you've been living up until this moment if that life isn't filled with love and positivity.

It's time to let go of the past.

I've judged myself for the vast majority of my life. I still struggle with it today. I post something and immediately judge myself. I wear something I'm unsure of and immediately judge myself. I decided to write this book and I judged myself. I teach people to stop judging themselves and yet I catch my mind doing it at times.

I know better now. I know to separate my thoughts into those that serve me and those that don't. I know to put myself first. I know that I'm worthy of my dreams, so I actively chase them. I know to accept only what will push me to be better and to let go of everyone and everything else that is holding me back.

You, too, will find yourself judging your actions and your ideas, even after knowing all of this. The funny things is, that it has always happened. The difference is that you know better now. You know how to be better. You know your worth. You know your beauty. You know what your dreams are. You are able to differentiate between those who support you and those who

I INVITE YOU TO RECITE THIS MANTRA EVERYDAY AS PART OF YOUR DAILY ROUTINE WHEN YOU ARE DECLARING WHAT YOU WANT TO THE UNIVERSE OR GOD: "THIS, OR SOMETHING BETTER" AND GO ON WITH YOUR PLANS KNOWING THE UNIVERSE HAS YOUR BACK.

only want to critique you. You are stronger than ever before because you are aware of your strength. It has always been there, but now you see it and accept it for all that it is.

You see yourself for all that you are and all that you know you can be. I see you, too. I see you going out and conquering the world in whatever way you dream, wherever that may be. If you made it this far in the book, I know that you are smart enough to believe in yourself, to trust yourself, to love yourself.

You can and will accomplish everything you set your mind to—even when you don't. Failure is never a thing. Even when we don't accomplish the things that we want when we want them, it could mean only that we are taking a longer road to our destination. Other times, it is the universe letting us know that it has a better plan for us.

I invite you to recite this mantra everyday as part of your daily routine when you are declaring what you want to the universe or God: "This, or something better" and go on with your plans knowing the universe has your back.

I've learned, painfully and slowly, to control my thoughts, and sometimes ignore them, through mindfulness and yoga. Yes, I know I love yoga like crazy, but the truth is, when you start to become more present in your days and in your life, you start to notice the thoughts as they come, so it becomes easier to catch any negative thought as soon as it shows up. I do what I've learned and shared with you. I stop, let the negative feelings be there for a couple of minutes, and then let them go.

You are worthy of your dreams. Always remember that. You are worthy of love and acceptance. Now, let go of everything that is not serving you and start building the life you deserve.

YOU ARE WORTHY OF YOUR DREAMS. ALWAYS REMEMBER THAT. YOU ARE WORTHY OF LOVE AND ACCEPTANCE. NOW, LET GO OF EVERYTHING THAT IS NOT SERVING YOU AND START BUILDING THE LIFE YOU DESERVE.

REBEL LIFESTYLE DESIGN STEP 3

TAKE ACTION

You're ready!! I'm so excited for you to be in this section right now and to start making the first changes in your life that will lead your days to being filled WITH UTTER HAPPINESS, SOUL FULFILLMENT, AND NOOOO SOCIETAL EXPECTATIONS MESSING WITH YOUR HEAD!!

Cheers to you, Girl, for arriving here!

You may have skipped all the way here from Chapter 1 or you may have read the whole thing until you arrived. The important thing is that you are reading this right now and have decided to put yourself first and to take action toward the life of your dreams!

I promise you right now, and feel free to call me on it if I don't deliver, that if you follow through with the 30 days, you'll take a look at yourself at the end and you won't believe the transformation you've made!

You'll feel so much love for yourself that it will be hard to imagine going back to a place of self-hate and people-pleasing.

You'll be surprised at how committed you are to your future and to achieving your goals. Like never before, that procrastination will elude you.

You won't even believe how much time and energy it took to be constantly judging others and yourself, to be complaining and criticizing, and how fast you are going to be able to notice the haters in your life as soon as they open their mouths. You'll seriously wish you'd started sooner!

I cross-my-heart-and-hope-to-die pinky-promise!

CHAPTER 16

Quick Tip Before We Get Started!

I do my entire life AROUND apps. Even writing this book almost happened on an app... however, I do like the keyboard of my lap   everything else happens on my phone.

I do yoga on an app and meditate on apps. I have a physical journal and planner and have their app counterparts that I take with me everywhere. I have affirmations on an app and even my meal plans happen on my phone! If you are 100% as tech dependent as I am, check out the Resources section where I give you all my app recommendations that I use on a daily basis plus a lot more fun stuff. ;)

You are ready to get started!

CHAPTER 17

Prep Work

This book has been laying the foundation for you to reconnect with yourself and discover what your soul is telling you before we move on to taking action on those desires and goals.

In order to conquer the world, we must first conquer ourselves.

In the next 30 days, you are going to work on improving yourself *and then* moving on to improve your life. It doesn't happen the other way around.

To get you ready for your action-packed second challenge, we are going to work on detoxifying your mind and body so the real you can come out and be ready for the next steps that will have you accomplishing goals on a daily basis.

YOU ARE GOING TO LEARN TO LOVE YOURSELF LIKE IT'S YOUR JOB WHILE ACCOMPLISHING ALL OF YOUR DREAMS KNOWING THAT YOU ARE 100% WORTHY OF THEM LIKE A TOTAL #GIRLBOSS!!

You are going to learn to LOVE YOURSELF LIKE IT'S YOUR JOB while accomplishing all of your dreams knowing that you are 100% worthy of them like a total #girlboss!! Enough talking. Let's start doing!

ACTION #1 – Download the workbook.

First things first. Go to *momisnotalwaysright.com/resources* and download your free copy of the challenge workbook where you have everything you need to clarify your intentions and spell out your affirmations. It's an easy fill-in-the-blanks file that will have you narrowing down your ideas and breaking down your dreams in a step-by-step guide. You'll go over your answers every day and it will seem like a breeze to follow through because it will all be in the same place! ☺

ACTION #2 – Do the workbook.

Duh! Block your time for the next hour, put this book down, and do the exercises in the workbook. Yes, NOW! Put the book down. I'll wait.

By setting this 30 – 60 minutes aside to do the work TODAY, you'll be ready to start your challenge tomorrow and you'll feel over-the-moon inspired to get started with your inner and outer transformation and with taking control of your life!

So... go ahead and complete it! You deserve those minutes of inner search!

Done? Good.

(BONUS) ACTION #3 – Join the community and get an accountability partner.

Research has shown time and time again that you are far more likely to accomplish any goal your set for yourself if you have some form of accountability. When we are talking about something as important as you living a life you love and accepting your body, mind, and life as a precious gift, that is something that you don't want to procrastinate!

I know I need some serious accountability to follow through, which is why I know what I'm talking about! Trust me. If you haven't already, head over to *momisnotalwaysright.com/resources* and ask to join the community.

As soon as you are in, read the rules, introduce yourself, and ask for an accountability partner! We will all be there ready to cheer you on during your journey, so you don't have to do this alone. We will make sure you are matched with an accountability partner so that both of you can hold each other accountable and achieve all that greatness that I know you can have! ☺

If you feel that you may prefer a person in your life to be your accountability partner instead, have that person head over to *momisnotalwaysright.com/resources* to download two free chapters of the book, a free workbook, and get everything needed to get started with you!

In any case, remember to start your challenge tomorrow regardless of having an accountability partner or not! Accountability partners can join you while you are on day 4, 5, 10, or even after you've already started your second challenge!

Sometimes we inspire those around us by making the changes in ourselves first. Become your girlfriends' role model and get started with your rebellion tomorrow!

CHAPTER 18

Challenge 1 –
The 30-Day Challenge

Now, armed with your workbook and your desire to live a life where you are the only one calling the shots and others' opinions simply don't matter, go ahead and start the challenge!!

For the next 30 days, you are going to increase your self-esteem. You are going to get a clear idea on where you want your life to go. You'll make sure never to forget again. Last, but not least, you are going create an amazing relationship with yourself that will push you to break any barrier that is currently in the way of your dream life.

From this moment forward, you are going to treat yourself like your best friend and soulmate. You'll only address yourself with kindness, compassion, and gratitude. More importantly, you won't let anyone who tries to put you down get away with it. You will block those people from your life. You have no time for haters.

RULES

1. **Take full responsibility for everything in your life.**

   Get your power back! Responsibility and blame are NOT the same. Whomever you think is at blame for anything in your life, it doesn't make it their responsibility to fix it. It is YOUR responsibility to do something about it. It's your life. You have the power to change anything in it, including how others make you feel or the situation you are in.

2. **No judging, criticizing, or complaining about anyone or anything—INCLUDING about yourself.**

   For the next 30 days, no more hate talks to yourself about how fat you look in those jeans, how stupid you are for not following through with your plans, or joining on the team's laughs about why that girl thinks she can pull off blonde.

NO JUDGING.

"WHAT WOULD THE PERSON I WANT TO BECOME DO IN THIS SITUATION?"

Respect everyone's right to do with his or her life what he or she wants. It would be the ultimate act of hypocrisy if you wanted to live life according to your rules, but you meddle in other people's when they are trying to do the same. If you want respect and no judgment, offer the same thing back. Always remember to think, "What would the person I want to become do in this situation?"

3. **Nothing but positivity out of your mouth.**

You may have been a glass-half-empty kind of girl up until this point, but by now you know that it takes the same amount of energy to focus on the problem as it does to focus on the solution. If you are too busy bitching about how bad traffic is, you'll miss the awesome opportunity to catch up on your podcasts! For the next 30 days, you'll say only positive things. More importantly, you'll say only the things that you want to become a reality. By actively stopping yourself from saying something you don't want, you'll be forced always to keep in mind what you truly want for your life and act on it!

4. **Take 10 minutes for yourself:**

a. **5 minutes to practice gratitude.**

Every morning, before checking your Instagram and Snapchat, you are going to take the FIRST FIVE minutes of the day, sitting down on your bed (or the toilet), and you are going to recite all the things you are grateful for starting with: having a new day, your body and the work it does for you, your abundance, your health, a job/car/roof over your head/real friends, and anything else you are grateful for. It's the small things that sometimes we take for granted that matter the most. Be grateful for every single one of them and experience in real-time how it changes the outcome of your day. Do this through prayer, meditation, or simply listing them in your head or saying them out loud. Extra points if you write them down!

b. **<1 minute to stand naked in front of the mirror and say "I Love You. You're beautiful."**

After you're done with your gratitude practice and are about to jump in the shower, take a minute to look at yourself in your birthday suit, look yourself in the eye, and say "I Love You." Look at the parts that you are not used to thinking are beautiful and say "You're beautiful. I love you and I'm grateful for the work you do." They need to hear it the most.

If a tear drops, you're only normal ;). This is a life-changing practice; I promise.

c.   <5 minutes to recite your affirmations.

You can do this still naked in the mirror. Grab your workbook (or the app of your choice) and recite the affirmations you created, including rules 1 – 3. This will help you stay on top of your goals, your daily tasks, and keep them always in your head as you move along your day. A goal that is not visible is a goal that won't get done.

5.   (BONUS) Stay accountable!

Either set a date with your accountability partner and make sure you are both following through and sharing each other's wins or share with us in the Community how you're doing! Let us know that you are ready to start the challenge and make sure to say #dayone at the beginning!! We want to know what day of the challenge you are on, what obstacles have you encountered, and how much you've already learned about yourself. We are eager to help, to keep you accountable, and more importantly, simply to be there for you if you ever need an escape from the harshness of everyday life a girl has to go through. Someone else may need some words of encouragement as well! Remember, there is almost nothing that you are going through that one of us has never been through before. Reach out! Make it a daily habit to post and you'll be amazed at how much easier the challenge will be! Especially the no judging rule—that one's tough!

That's it. Five easy steps that take almost no time, but do take some courage and serious self-love. They will shift the way you think and feel about yourself and your current life while laying a strong foundation for starting the rebellion we discuss in Section 2. Ultimately, you will enjoy every single one of your days as a confident, self-made woman who is not only *not afraid*, but is passionately motivated to follow her dreams.

Unstoppable and unapologetic: these are your new adjectives ;).

CHAPTER 19

Challenge 2 – Three Steps To The Life Of Your Dreams

G irl, self-love is the new black and you are all styled up! You have come such a wonderful long way to get here. I have to confess; I'm getting teared up imagining you about to embark on your own path toward your dream life. You have learned so much over the past days and I wish you could just take a moment to stop, breathe, and thank yourself for all the work you have done so far, for everything that you've learned, and for everything that you have discovered.

You are such a different person from who you were at the beginning of this book, yet somehow you are just the same, except more *you* than ever. You ARE your *youest* you possible.

I love you for that. I love everything you've done and everything you've yet to accomplish. I am cheering you on. Always remember, even in those darker days, that I believe in you. I see you. I know you are worth it. You've got this.

I LOVE EVERYTHING YOU'VE DONE AND EVERYTHING YOU'VE YET TO ACCOMPLISH. I AM CHEERING YOU ON. ALWAYS REMEMBER, EVEN IN THOSE DARKER DAYS, THAT I BELIEVE IN YOU. I SEE YOU. I KNOW YOU ARE WORTH IT. YOU'VE GOT THIS.

This new challenge is about changing your life—NOW—with real actionable steps that will actually cause a difference on what happens in your everyday life.

We started the first challenge by making sure to set the foundation for your best life: accepting your body, accepting your ideas as doable, and accepting your mind as something beautiful. You know better now. You know how beautiful you are, how perfect your body is—just as it is—and you know that life will never be the same because of what you've learned.

Now let's dive right in with your new 30-day challenge that is about to propel your life forward in ways you have yet to see. Hold on tight, pour yourself a bubbly drink, and let's get going!

PREP

If you still haven't done the exercises, please head on over to *momisnotalwaysright.com/resources* to download them and start filling in the blanks so you have an exact action plan for your dreams! Set aside a good hour or two to get them done. This is the foundation for your dream life!

Already have them? Cheers to that! Let's keep going!

Step 1. Continue Your 1st Challenge for the Next 30 Days

It is meant to be a practice for life. Why would you want to stop letting yourself know what you are grateful for, how beautiful you are, and why you are doing the things you are doing? More importantly, why would you ever want to stop showering yourself with love each morning? You don't and you won't. Not for at least the next 30 days—hopefully never.

Practice gratitude every morning. Recite your affirmations. Add your revised WHY while standing naked in front of the mirror. Stop judging others. Stop judging yourself. Treat your body like a temple at all times.

Those sacred 10 minutes in the morning have changed your life and will continue to do so, hopefully for the rest of your life. I have practiced them for over two years. The days I don't do them, my days pretty easily turn to bad days and are simply not as happy and fulfilling as the days I do them. Being grateful, feeling beautiful, and knowing what your life is all about are the keys to happiness! Never let those habits disappear! Why would you ever want to feel anything different?

Step 2. Set aside 30 – 90 minutes of SACRED TIME FOR 30 DAYS to do your daily tasks.

This is the time that you will use to work on the daily tasks that you created on your DESIGN A LIFE YOU LOVE workbook. This time HAS TO BE considered sacred: no interruptions and no distractions. Your whole life depends on it. Remember that you are worthy of your dreams and they are worthy of your time.

Refer to the "Make Time" section in Chapter 9 to know how to craft this time. Think on your commute. Think in the morning. Think on Sundays. Think in the afternoon. Re-read Chapter 9 and find what works for you! I suggest 30 – 90 minutes per day five days a week, but you can also batch your activities and do them all on #selfcaresunday which also works incredibly! I've tried both and they are both powerful. For me, though, daily activities that push me forward have turned out to be more effective. Find what works for you!

Remember, you can always find excuses. Recite your WHY every morning to destroy excuses. Your WHY will give you the right REASON to succeed at this. Put them on your schedule WITHOUT the possibility of SNOOZE. This will help procrastination stay at bay. When you feel procrastination crawling in, re-read the "Procrastination" section in Chapter 13 and get actionable tips for conquering it every time!

You know exactly what to do each day. This will make it infinitely more effective to get this done!

Step 3. Cut Negative People for the Next 30 Days

It's important to set yourself up for success by surrounding yourself with people who want to see you succeed. I have been insisting since day one that you should block those people who don't get what you are doing or who don't have your best interests in mind. For this challenge, you will do exactly that.

If you haven't already, for the next 30 days, cut your communication with everyone who pushes you down, who cause doubts in you, who robs you of your good energy, or who truly doesn't want to see you defy the status quo because it threatens the way he or she lives. For the next 30 days, these people won't be a part of your life.

Think of it like a detox for your mind and soul.

No calling. No texting. No going out for drinks. No gossiping with them or about them. Remove them from your social media. Create a new Instagram—anything you need. If they call, tell them you are busy. If they want you to join them at a bar, tell them you have work. Simply be unavailable for them for the next 30 days. Be RUTHLESS!

Remember to be mindful and to follow your instincts on who to trust and who not to trust.

You know who they are. You have discovered exactly who these people are. You have the skills to stay away, if only for the next 30 days. You will spend all your energy and time focusing on changing your life and you can't have them trying to put more burden on you.

After you finish the 30 days of this challenge, it is another good time to recognize who your tribe really is. Rely on your tribe—your like-minded peeps who, just like you, want to make their lives whatever they dream. Rely on the people you tell your wildest desires to who, instead of thinking you are crazy or that it's impossible, ask, "What are you waiting for?" Hold them tight and never let go! Remember this can be online, offline, or both. Whatever works for you.

Remember that we are here for you as well in our like-minded community! Tag us or join us. We are always here to cheer you on. You don't have to go through this alone.

Post daily for us so we can see you in action changing your life! Use the hashtag #rebellifestyledesign and we will be there supporting you!

Extra Step: CELEBRATE!

You deserve it. You are worth it. It is almost magical how different and yet the same you are. Life is finally a happy dream. You finally feel happiness for your day and everything in it. I'm proud of you. You should celebrate!

Take a moment and acknowledge how far you've come. You've made progress, even on the days you feel you didn't accomplish what you were supposed to, you showed up and that is to be celebrated.

Cheers to you choosing to live a life YOU love! *clink* *clink*

Welcome to the #rebellifestyledesign club ;)

WORKBOOK

CALENDAR

My Big Goal:

GOALS:
1-
2- *Daily affirmations*
3- *Detox*

MONDAY	TUESDAY	WEDNESDAY	THURSDAY	FRIDAY	SATURDAY	SUNDAY	WEEKLY GOALS
1 2 3	1 2 3	1 2 3	1 2 3	1 2 3	1 2 3	REVIEW	1- 2- *Affirmations* 3 - *7 day detox*
2 3	1 2 3	1 2 3	1 2 3	1 2 3	1 2 3	REVIEW	1- 2- *Affirmations* 3 - *7 day detox*
1 2 3	1 2 3	1 2 3	1 2 3	1 2 3	1 2 3	REVIEW	1- 2- *Affirmations* 3 - *7 day detox*
1 2 3	1 2 3	1 2 3	1 2 3	1 2 3	1 2 3	REVIEW	1- 2- *Affirmations* 3 - *7 day detox*
1 2 3	1 2 3	1 2 3	1 2 3	1 2 3	1 2 3	REVIEW	1- 2- *Affirmations* 3 - *7 day detox*

I'm capable, authentic, beautiful and enough, just as I am.

CHAPTER 20

Bonus – Got More Time?

Well *Hello There,* Overachiever!!

If you are anything like me, not only did you download the workbook on cue, but you already did all the exercises and are now reading this bonus chapter to see what else is there to do! Well if you are here now, that means that you are ready to live the life you've always imagined and you are not willing to waste another day trying to prove to others that you can or can't do anything.

You are ready to take back control of your life and to plan your future according to what YOUR HEART truly desires! If that is the case, and you are willing to set aside more time for you and do more while still committing to the 30 days, here are some optional awesome practices you can follow to shift your life almost overnight!

Start an Exercise Routine

As you know, when it comes to exercising, yoga is my drug! It really makes my body feel incredible during and after each practice. I can literally feel it healing my body after a long day. If that is something you want to try, go ahead and see how you feel! If yoga is not doing it for you though, pick an activity that gives your mind and body the break they deserve from being awesome all day. They are begging for it!! Even if you can only fit in five minutes a day, it can really improve your day! From sun-salutations to a quick sprint or even jumping jacks in the morning to help you get your heart rate up. It will give you an awesome energy burst that will motivate you to start your day right.

Meditate

The power of daily meditation has been proven time and time again; it is no surprise that it is an important part of the daily routines of highly successful people. I personally find it grounding and extremely helpful when my mind is all over the place and I need to stop and remember what is truly important and how I'm feeling during the day. One time, I got so focused on my meditation practice that I literally felt my soul. I realized that my body is just this awesome home I inhabit and my true self is within this beautiful vessel.

When I opened my eyes, I had a renewed respect for my body that pushed me to appreciate it and love it every single day. It was truly a groundbreaking experience and it happened during a 10-minute meditation on my sofa! Meditation makes me find a connection with myself by quieting down everything and everyone around me to give room for my thoughts and inner desires to come to the surface. Try it. Begin with a couple of minutes and work your way up to 10 or more!

Gratitude Journal

Grab a new journal and name it your gratitude journal. Use it to list all the things you are grateful for every day, or at any moment during the day. You can also use it to dump all the thoughts in your head to help you clarify your ideas. This is an incredible way to track the awesome progress you'll make in the next few days as you notice your ideas evolving! I've been journaling for years. Since I started doing a gratitude journal, it really helps putting everything else around me in perspective by starting my day feeling grateful.

Do a 360 Detox

Detoxes have been popular for a long time. That is because the logic behind them works. Take a few days to eat almost nothing so your body can get rid of the buildup, hit a reset button, and then start all over again. It's like when you clean your make up brushes, but for your body.

The detox I'm proposing, however, is not just for your body. It is also for your mind and social interactions. For your body, try a detox to start new and refreshed. Anything from simply removing junk food for the next 30 days to doing a full-on juice cleanse for 7 days—whatever feels right for you and your body. I suggest at least removing all processed foods for a month and you'll be amazed at how your body feels. Give your body some love!

For your mind, detox your environment, including social media. Remove anything from your environment or anyone from social media that causes negative feelings in you. Unfollow the haters, the posers, the conflictive, and the people who impose stereotypes you are not buying into anymore. Follow accounts that inspire you, that truly motivate you—role models and true friends.

Declutter your house from all the stuff that you no longer have any use for that is only taking up space and collecting dust.

Hang up new uplifting art, pictures of your loved ones, get a new scented candle, or try aromatherapy.

Make sure that when you log in to Instagram or walk into your house, you feel safe, empowered, and motivated.

For your social interactions, take the time really to ask yourself, "Who values my time?" Take what you've learned from this book and analyze the people you're spending your time with. Discover who is adding value to your life and who is just robbing you of your energy and time.

Who are your peeps with whom you can be completely yourself? Who is 100% behind your quest to conquer the world? Who is there only to see you fail? Avoid all contact with the latter for the next 30 days—hopefully forever.

Read!

Reading dramatically change my life a few years ago. Back then, I was your typical girl: running around doing me, considering myself a hardcore night owl, always feeling like there weren't enough hours in the day.... Then I came across a book that talked about the benefits of mornings, and I decided to give it a try just for a change.

Part of the morning routine the book proposed was to use 10 minutes to read something else. This proved to change everything in my life.

I read another book that taught me the power of passive income and living life fully on your terms...

Then I read another book on how to set goals that align with who you are and your passions...

Then I read another book on how to stop worrying about what other people think...

You can see where I'm going with this. Reading fully and completely changed my life, my views on the world, and eventually led me to write MY own book. Yes, if you are committed to living your best life, I definitely recommend you start reading—even if it's 10 minutes a day.

If you are like me and find yourself stuck in traffic most days, download an app to listen to books instead of having to read them. It has saved me tons of hours and I have been able to "read" so many more books, all the while improving my own life and giving intention to my time behind the wheel. For my recommended reading list, and links directing you to the books' sites head over to Chapter 21: Resources.

Read on!

While these awesome extra practices will cause a major shift in your life, remember that they are optional on the challenge. You are free to pick as few or as many as you want, or none at all! If you do choose to add this to your personal challenge, you are committing to it for the whole 30 days, not just for a couple of days.

Discipline is key to achieving any goal. This is no different. I know that procrastination is not your thing because you read this book all the way to here and are extremely excited to get started!

In any case, I use an awesome app for my morning routine that keeps me in check with what I need to do in the right order so I'm always nailing it. Check it out in the Resources chapter.

Now, go ahead, you beautiful #rebel. Take a look and choose what resonates with you! Tomorrow, you'll #designalifeyoulove and I'm bursting with excitement for you!! Remember to share with me how you're doing! Post in the community daily so I know how awesome your progress is!

See you on the other side! ☺

CHAPTER 21

Resources

Note: Some of these links are affiliate links. This means I get a percentage of your purchase if you buy though my links. By buying through these links, you are actively supporting my mission to empower women all over the world to break free from societal expectations and follow their dreams.

Physical Journal/Agenda

Daily journal I use: Daily or Weekly Planner by Danielle LaPorte: *http://bit.ly/332wYoM*

Great journal I've used for goal tracking: BEST Journal: *http://bit.ly/2osTEzs*

App I use when traveling or out and about: 5-minute journal app

Meditation

Insight Timer: *https://insighttimer.com*

Calm: *https://www.calm.com* (I love their music as background when working)

Headspace (for beginners): *https://www.headspace.com*

Meditation Cushion (the one I use): *https://amzn.to/31XRGVF*

Yoga

Yoga Studio App: *https://www.yogastudioapp.com* (I use it almost daily)

Live Kundalini: *https://www.kundalinilive.com* (Trying it out)

Yoga mat (the one I use): *https://amzn.to/2WooLsB*

Accounts to Follow

Mine: @thekendraaraujo - https://www.instagram.com/thekendraaraujo/

BOPO and crazy dances: @bodiposipanda - *https://www.instagram.com/bodyposipanda/*

BOPO and fatactivism: @iamdaniadriana - *https://www.instagram.com/iamdaniadriana/*

BOPO and real: @nurishandeat - *https://www.instagram.com/nourishandeat/*

Follow accounts that encourage you to be better, to be yourself, or are doing what you aspire to accomplish.

Books I've read and recommend

The Desire Map by Danielle Laporte: *https://amzn.to/2NrDPSO*

The Universe Has Your Back by Gabrielle Bernstein: *https://amzn.to/2ouRakf*

The Game of Life And How To Play It by Florence Scovel Shinn: *https://amzn.to/322p9hL*

The Happiness Plan by Dr. Elise Bialylew: *https://amzn.to/345jhpg*

Body Positive Power by Megan Jayne Crabbe: *https://amzn.to/2q8Gc47*

The Miracle Morning by Hal Elrod: *https://amzn.to/2NlRSlV*

The Subtle Art of Not Giving A F*ck by Mark Manson: *https://amzn.to/31Tj1bf*

Published by Chandler Bolt: *https://amzn.to/2qVsWjW*

The 4 Hour Work Week by Tim Ferris: *https://amzn.to/34dSqqW*

#Girlboss by Sophia Amoruso: *https://amzn.to/2XwcqD8*

CHAPTER 22

One Last Thing...

You know, Rebel, at this point I consider us long-lost friends. I mean, if after sharing my entire life worth of embarrassing stories, you don't think you know me well enough to like me... I'm going to bet that you do and that you consider me your long-lost friend too.

Being friends, I want to ask you for one last thing as you continue creating the rebel life you deserve. Help me do the same for other women around the world by sparing two minutes of your time.

Please follow this link and let the world know what you think of this book and how our friendship has changed your outlook of the world:

momisnotalwaysright.com/review

You have no idea the huge favor you would be doing all the women who will be able to find this book in the never-ending online world thanks to your review and how my heart is jumping up and down with joy for your kindness.

Please visit *momisnotalwaysright.com/review* and let other women know what you think of the book!

Friend, thank you for your two minutes. As always, cheers to you. *clink* *clink*

REFERENCES

Oprah Bio - *https://www.imdb.com/name/nm0001856/bio*

Jeff Hoffman Bio - *https://www.startlandnews.com/2016/09/look-into-priceline-founder-jeff-hoffmans-toolkit-of-inspiration/*

Katy Perry Bio - *https://www.biography.com/musician/katy-perry*

ABOUT THE AUTHOR

Kendra Araujo is an interior and rebel lifestyle designer, author, speaker, and world traveler who helps women break free from societal expectations to design their dream lives.

After fulfilling her lifelong dream of traveling the world and visiting over 35 countries in under two years, Kendra took a break from her successful interior design firm—against everyone else's advice—to help others achieve their dreams like she has achieved hers.

Self-proclaimed "rebel and free," Kendra wrote the book *Mom is Not Always Right* and founded Rebel Lifestyle Academy to empower women in their 20s, 30s, and beyond to follow their dreams, even if they go against their family's or society's expectations.

Besides her Bachelor Degree in Interior Design, Kendra has completed the Science of Well-being course from Yale University. She is a certified wellness coach, a Rebel-lifestyle Designer, and the host of the "Rebel and Live Your Dream Life" podcast with thousands of downloads.

She has *now* been to almost 50 countries and holds online courses and in-person workshops globally helping hundreds of women get closer to their dream life by following her step-by-step process. She has appeared on TV, radio, and podcasts internationally.

You can find her rocking her signature blonde curls, traveling in style with her husband, doing yoga, or volunteering at local charities.

We have a gift for you!

20% OFF
your order

Beautiful rebel I have one more gift for you. Because you are here, reading this book and taking these steps that will get you to the life you want to live, here is a 20% OFF code for you to continue your journey with us.

Simply go to **www.KendraAraujo.com/theacademy** and apply it to any of our courses, meditations or workshops!

CODE: **MINARFRIENDS**

Made in the USA
Columbia, SC
19 February 2021

33220974R00226